EMOTIONAL EATING

WHY You Do It & HOW To Beat It

Practical Tools To Break Free From Bingeing, Overcome Emotional Triggers, Start Loving Yourself and Discover A Happier You!

KITTY BARRETT

© **Copyright Kitty Barrett 2024 - All rights reserved.**

All rights reserved.

The content within this book may not be reproduced, duplicated or transmitted without direct written permission from the author or the publisher, except as permitted by U.S. copyright law.

Under no circumstances will any blame or legal responsibility be held against the publisher, or author, for any damages, reparation, or monetary loss due to the information contained within this book. Either directly or indirectly. You are responsible for your own choices, actions, and results.

Legal Notice:

This book is copyright protected. This book is only for personal use. You cannot amend, distribute, sell, use, quote or paraphrase any part of the content within this book, without the consent of the author or publisher.

Disclaimer Notice:

Please note that the information contained within this document is for educational and entertainment purposes only. All effort has been expended to present accurate, up-to-date, and reliable, complete information. No warranties of any kind are declared or implied. Readers acknowledge that the author is not engaging in the rendering of legal, financial, medical or professional advice. The content within this book has been derived from various sources. Please consult a licensed professional before attempting any techniques outlined in this book.

By reading this document, the reader agrees that under no circumstances is the author responsible for any losses, direct or indirect, which are incurred as a result of the use of the information contained within this document, including, but not limited to, — errors, omissions, or inaccuracies.

A SPECIAL GIFT FOR YOU

Thank you for getting a copy of my book - your kind support means a lot to me. As a token of my appreciation, I would like to give you a FREE digital copy of "Live Love Laugh: Affirmation & Gratitude Journal"

To get your copy, simply scan the QR code or visit the link below:

https://bit.ly/free-livejournal

Contents

Introduction		1
1.	Emotional Eating - Why We Do It	3
	1.1 Emotional Hunger vs. Physical Hunger: Recognizing the Differences	
	1.2 The Science of Stress Eating & Bingeing: What Happens in Your Brain	
	1.3 Emotional Eating Across Life's Stages	
	1.4 The Role of Society and Media in Shaping Our Eating Habits	
2.	Identifying Your Emotional Triggers	14
	2.1 The Most Common Emotional Trigger and How to Spot Them	
	2.2 The Link Between Emotional Eating and Unmet Emotional Needs or Past Trauma	

- 2.3 Food as Comfort: Why We Turn to Eating in Times of Emotional Turmoil
- 2.4 Stress, Anxiety, and Boredom: A Triad of Emotional Eating
- 2.5 Using a Food and Mood Diary to Uncover Your Emotional Eating Patterns

3. Emotional Eating - How To Beat It   31
  - 3.1 The Power of Mindful Eating
  - 3.2 Mindful Eating in Practice: Strategies for Everyday Meals
  - 3.3 Relearning Hunger and Fullness Cues
  - 3.4 Combining Mindfulness with Emotional Awareness for Lasting Change
  - 3.5 The 4-Step S-T-O-P Method
  - 3.6 How To Manage Emotional Eating

4. Transforming Your Relationship with Food   62
  - 4.1 How to Enjoy All Foods Without Guilt or Bingeing

- 4.2 Intuitive Eating: Listening to Your Body's Needs
- 4.3 The Importance of Nutritional Balance and Variety
- 4.4 Healthy Eating Hacks: Mind Over Meals
- 4.5 Replacing Emotional Eating Habits with Nourishing Practices
- 4.6 Celebrating Food: Creating New, Positive Food Memories

5. The Role of Body Image in Emotional Eating — 81
   - 5.1 Unpacking the Impact of Body Image on Eating Habits
   - 5.2 Cultivating Body Positivity and Self-Acceptance
   - 5.3 The Media and Body Image: Developing Critical Viewing Skills
   - 5.4 Body Image Healing Practices: From Affirmations to Self-Care Routines

6. Building a Toolkit for Emotional Resilience — 95

    6.1 Your Emotions Without Food

    6.2 Mindfulness Practices for Interrupting Emotional Eating Episodes

    6.3 The Power of Movement & Exercise in Emotional Well-Being

    6.4 Cultivating Self-Compassion & Self-Care: A Journey to Self-Love

    6.5 Strategies for Managing Emotional Eating Without Dieting

7. Overcoming Setbacks and Maintaining Progress — 113

    7.1 Identifying and Learning from Emotional Eating Setbacks

    7.2 The Role of Self-Compassion in Overcoming Guilt and Shame

    7.3 Keeping a Progress Journal: Celebrating Successes, Big and Small

    7.4 Setting Boundaries Around Food

	7.5	Creating a Supportive Eating Environment	
	7.6	Adjusting Your Strategy As Life Changes	
	7.7	Building a Long-Term Support Network & Community	
8.		Lifestyle Changes For Long-Term Success	138
	8.1	Integrating Healthy Eating into a Balanced Lifestyle	
	8.2	Sleep: The Unsung Hero in Managing Emotional Eating	
	8.3	Time Management Strategies for Stress Reduction	
	8.4	Setting Goals for the Future: Beyond Emotional Eating	
	8.5	The Quick-Start 1-Week Mindful Eating Meal Plan	
	8.6	Holistic Approach to Healing	

9.		Happier Life Beyond Emotional Eating	159
	9.1	Embracing Change: The Journey of Self-Discovery and Growth	
	9.2	Beyond the Book: Continuing Your Journey Toward a Happier You	
Conclusion			165
References			167

Introduction

Have you ever found yourself standing in front of the refrigerator, door ajar, feeling that familiar tug of needing something to fill a void, but not quite knowing what it is? You're not really hungry, but you're reaching for something that feels like comfort, like a silent friend in moments of stress, sadness or anxiety. If this scene feels uncomfortably familiar, you're not alone.

My own moment of clarity came from one chilly evening after a particularly stressful work meeting. I was knee-deep in family responsibilities, barely balancing my career and personal life, and there I was — raiding the kitchen, looking for something to soothe the mounting pressure. It wasn't until I found myself devouring a large slice of leftover cake, barely tasting it — that I realized I wasn't eating out of hunger but out of need for comfort and control.

Abandoned as a child, I know that apart from having to deal with day-to-day stressors, I was also affected by the burden of my childhood trauma. I share this with you because I believe many of you have had similar experiences, and it's time we understand the intricate dance between our emotions and eating habits. So, let's tackle this challenge together.

This book is a passage into understanding why we turn to food when our emotions run high and how we can forge a new path to nourishing our body and soul without guilt or regret. In these pages, we will explore the root cause of emotional eating, equip ourselves with tools and strategies to conquer it, and make long-term sustainable changes.

Unlike other books that offer quick fixes, this book takes a unique approach, focusing on long-term, sustainable healing. Each chapter is designed to actively engage you in your healing process through practical exercises, quizzes, and actionable advice to bring you closer to the core of your eating habits, understand them, and transform them. You'll also find a quick-start 1-week mindful meal plan to ease you into a healthier eating routine and start a new phase of your life.

This is your invitation to break free from the cycle of emotional eating. Together, we'll uncover the emotional triggers that lead to binge eating, discover comfort that doesn't rely on food and tackle body image issues head-on. By the end of this book, you will have more than just knowledge; you will experience a profound shift in how you relate to food and your emotions. You will come away empowered, with a renewed joy in your life and the tools to maintain it.

This journey is about you discovering the strength and love within yourself to help you build a healthier, happier life. You have the power to transform your relationship with food and with yourself — YOU have control of your life.

Chapter 1
Emotional Eating - Why We Do It

"Life doesn't get easier or more forgiving, we get stronger and more resilient."

~ Steve Maraboli

Have you experienced a sudden, inexplicable urge to eat a specific food — and found yourself munching through a bag of chips or digging into a tub of ice cream without really being hungry? It's as if your hand has a mind of its own, reaching for comfort in food. Most of us have been there, and while it might feel like a quirky habit, it often signals something deeper: emotional hunger.

This chapter is about understanding the fine line between eating because you're physically hungry and eating to satisfy an emotional need. Recognizing the difference is your first step toward building a healthy relationship with food.

1.1 Emotional Hunger vs. Physical Hunger: Recognizing the Differences

Defining Emotional Hunger

Emotional hunger isn't about the body needing energy; it's about the mind seeking relief. It springs from feelings rather than from an empty stomach. You might crave specific comfort foods — think chocolates, salty snacks, or whatever your 'go-to' might be. These cravings are intense and feel urgent. Emotional hunger wants satisfaction now and won't settle for a carrot stick when it wants a chocolate bar. It's tied closely to feelings of reward and pleasure, making you feel momentarily happy but often leaves you with guilt or regret.

Contrasting Physical Hunger

Conversely, physical hunger is the body's straightforward signal that it's time to refuel. It builds gradually and will accept a variety of foods, not just the salty or sweet cravings associated with emotional hunger. Physical hunger is patient and can wait a bit until you find something nutritious to eat. Eating based on physical hunger makes you more likely to stop when you're full, avoiding that uncomfortably stuffed feeling that can follow an emotional eating spree.

Are You Experiencing Emotional Eating?

Recognizing emotional eating patterns involves noticing different signs and behaviors. Here are the three cues that include instances where you find yourself turning to food as a way to cope with stress, boredom, sadness, or other negative emotions rather than eating in response to physical hunger cues. You may also notice a pattern of overeating or binge eating during times of emotional distress, using food as a form of comfort or distraction from difficult feelings.

1. **Eating in Response to Emotions:** One big sign of emotional eating is eating because of your feelings instead of actual hunger. This includes eating when feeling stressed, anxious, sad, bored, or even happy. If you notice a regular pattern of using food to cope with emotions, it could mean you're affected by emotional eating.

2. **Consuming Comfort Foods:** Emotional eaters often gravitate towards specific foods known as comfort foods. Generally, such foods are high in fat, sugar, or carbohydrates and are associated with feelings of comfort, pleasure, or nostalgia. Noticing a preference for indulgent, high-calorie foods during times of emotional distress can be a sign of emotional eating.

3. **Mindless or Unconscious Eating:** Emotional eaters may engage in mindless or unconscious eating behaviors, such as eating quickly without paying attention to hunger cues, eating in front of the TV or computer, or snacking without being aware of portion sizes. These behaviors often involve a lack of mindfulness and awareness around eating, which can contribute to overeating and emotional eating patterns.

Emotional vs. Physical Hunger Quiz

To help you put what you've learned into practice, here's a quick quiz to gauge whether you're more likely to experience emotional hunger.

Reflect on your last eating experience and answer the following questions:

- Did I eat quickly, without paying attention to the taste or texture of the food?

- Was I craving a specific type of food (e.g., sweets, salty snacks) rather than feeling hungry for a proper balanced meal?

- Did my hunger come on suddenly, without any physical signs like stomach growling?

- Did I keep eating even when I no longer found the food satisfying, or did I eat past the point of feeling full or satisfied?

- Did I eat to distract myself from uncomfortable feelings or thoughts?

If you answered 'yes' to most of these questions, you might have been responding to emotional hunger. Recognizing this pattern is your initial step toward change. Remember, each meal is a new opportunity to practice mindful eating and build your understanding of your body's needs.

1.2 The Science of Stress Eating & Bingeing: What Happens in Your Brain

When you've had a long day filled with back-to-back meetings, unexpected bills to pay, or perhaps one of those days when everything seems to go wrong. How often do you find yourself reaching for something sweet or indulging in a fast food run? It's not just about willpower; there's a whole orchestra playing in your brain, making those fries and chocolate bars almost irresistible. Let's break down what's happening inside your brain when stress kicks in and why those comfort foods seem like such a good idea at that moment.

In this exploration, we dive into the intriguing world of emotional eating and unravel the scientific mechanisms behind our food choices linked to our emotions. From brain chemistry and hormonal responses to psychological triggers and neural pathways, a wealth of science influences how we eat during emotional moments.

Understanding the science behind emotional eating isn't just about unraveling mysteries; it's about empowering ourselves with knowledge and insights.

First, when stress enters the scene, your body reacts as though it's under attack and releases a wave of cortisol, known as the stress hormone. This hormone triggers a flood of glucose, supplying an immediate energy source to large muscles while inhibiting insulin production to prevent glucose from being stored. Cortisol's role extends beyond simply handling stress; it also increases appetite and can specifically heighten cravings for foods high in fat and sugar.

Eating these comfort foods with high fat and sugar activates the brain's reward system, and they trigger the release of dopamine — it is a neurotransmitter that makes us feel good. It's a short-term fix that ignites the brain's pleasure epicenters — such as winning a jackpot or getting a 'like' on social media. It's momentarily soothing and offers a psychological escape from stress. However, the relief is fleeting, and a cycle of emotional eating often follows because the brain starts associating these comfort foods with a quick, albeit temporary, fix for stress.

Over time, this behavior can reshape the landscape of your brain. With repeated activation, the brain's reward system becomes skewed, and eating these types of food shifts from a mere response to stress to an ingrained habit.

This change, known as neural plasticity, means that the brain starts reinforcing emotional eating behaviors, making them harder to break. Each cycle of stress eating further entrenches these pathways, making the pull of emotional eating even stronger each time stress rears its head.

The following further explains the scientific aspects of emotional eating and the complex interplay between emotions, psychology, physiology, and eating behaviors.

Neurobiology of Emotional Eating:

When we are stressed or feeling down, we tend to crave certain foods. Research in neurobiology suggests that specific brain regions, like the prefrontal cortex and the nucleus accumbens influence emotional eating. These regions are like the conductors of our food cravings orchestra — they regulate our mood, cravings, and motivation to eat. So, when we're feeling low, our brain's reward system may nudge us towards those comforting treats for a temporary mood boost.

Hormonal Regulation: The Stress-Hunger Connection:

Hormones are the silent influencers of our eating habits. Cortisol, known as the stress hormone, and ghrelin, the hunger hormone, can team up to influence our emotional eating behaviors. Picture this: when we're under chronic stress, our cortisol levels can soar, leading to increased cravings, especially for those high-calorie, feel-good foods. It's like our body's way of seeking comfort during tough times.

Emotional Regulation and Coping Mechanisms:

Using food as a coping mechanism is common when dealing with emotions like stress, anxiety, sadness, or even boredom. It's like reaching for a cookie or a bowl of ice cream to soothe the soul momentarily. However, it's important to note that this relief is temporary, and finding healthier coping strategies is key to long-term emotional well-being.

Psychological Factors: Unpacking the Mind-Body Connection:

Our minds play a crucial role in how we eat. Psychological factors like mood disorders, body image dissatisfaction, low self-esteem, and past trauma can all contribute to emotional eating tendencies. Understanding and addressing these underlying factors can be a significant stride toward liberating yourself from emotional eating patterns.

Social and Environmental Influences: Navigating the Food Landscape:

Our social and environmental surroundings also play a part in shaping our eating behaviors. Cultural norms, family dynamics, peer influences, and food availability all contribute to our relationship with food. Being mindful of these influences can help us make conscious choices aligned with our well-being goals.

Interoceptive Awareness: Tuning into Your Body's Signals:

Interoceptive awareness is about tuning into our body's internal cues, like hunger, fullness, and emotions. For example, meditation, deep breathing *(refer to chapter 3.4)* and mindful eating practices can enhance this awareness, helping us make more informed choices and reduce emotional eating tendencies. These tools and strategies will be discussed in detail in the upcoming chapters.

Understanding the intricate science behind emotional eating helps us make informed choices, break away from the cycle, and embark on a journey of self-discovery and healing. By nurturing a deeper awareness of our brain's workings, and all the aspects mentioned above, we can cultivate healthier relationships with food, emotions, and ourselves. It's a journey of resilience, compassion, and growth — one where each step forward brings us closer to a balanced, nourished, and fulfilling life.

1.3 Emotional Eating Across Life's Stages

When you consider the vast landscape of a woman's life, it's clear that each phase brings unique challenges and transitions — each capable of stirring the pot of emotional eating. From the excitement and nerves of starting college to the profound life-altering experience of becoming a mother, these transitions can sometimes send us straight into the comforting arms of our favorite foods.

It's not just about the stress of changes, though. Each stage of a woman's life is accompanied by significant physical and hormonal shifts that can influence her eating behaviors and emotional health.

Let's discuss those changes and how they align with our eating habits. Starting college or entering the workforce introduces a new level of independence and decision-making, including decisions about what, when, and how we eat. The freedom to choose can sometimes lead to stress eating, as food choices often double as emotional responses to new pressures and anxieties. Fast forward to motherhood, and you're navigating not just a new identity but also an entirely new body dynamic.

Adapting your eating habits and strategies to suit each life stage is crucial. For example, preparing simple, nutritious meals in advance during high-stress periods like college exams or significant work deadlines can prevent last-minute unhealthy eating.

As you transition into different roles — becoming a parent or entering the later stages of adulthood, educating yourself about your nutritional needs and emotional well-being can empower you to make choices that align with your body's changing requirements.

Pregnancy demands more of you nutritionally and emotionally. The body's increased need for nutrients can sometimes manifest in strong cravings, which are perfectly normal but can feel overwhelming. It's essential during these times to listen to your body, understand what it truly needs, and try to find a balance between satisfying cravings and maintaining nutritious eating habits.

TIPS Pregnancy is a dance of give and take with your body. Managing cravings isn't about denying yourself the chocolate or chips you might suddenly want; it's about understanding moderation and balance. A good strategy is to pair the object of your craving with something nutritious. Craving ice cream? Serve a smaller portion alongside a bowl of fresh fruit. It's about meeting your body halfway, ensuring that you're feeding it well while respecting its needs and desires during this critical time.

As we move toward menopause, the body again throws us a curveball with fluctuating hormones that can affect our appetite and weight. These changes can be frustrating and sometimes lead to emotional eating in order to cope with the body's unpredictability and the emotions that come with this new stage of life. It's beneficial during menopause to keep a food diary to track what you eat and how it makes you feel.

By doing this, it can help you identify patterns and triggers for emotional eating, allowing you to develop strategies to cope with them. Increasing your physical activity can also help manage weight and improve your mood, countering some of the physical and emotional challenges menopause brings.

Each stage of life might need a slightly different approach to managing emotional eating. Every phase of life offers a new opening for growth and understanding. By embracing these changes and responding to them with informed, compassionate responses, you can maintain a positive attitude toward food, which will support your physical and emotional well-being. This is not just about navigating the challenges but also about celebrating the body's incredible journey and capacities at every stage.

1.4 The Role of Society and Media in Shaping Our Eating Habits

It's almost impossible to watch TV, scroll through social media, or flip through a magazine without encountering relentless messages about what our bodies should look like and what we should eat. These messages often promote a narrow and unrealistic standard of beauty and health, which can profoundly impact our perspective of food and our body.

The pervasive diet culture, with its glorification of thinness and vilification of certain foods, sets a stage where food becomes not just about nutrition or pleasure but a battleground of willpower and morality.

Diet culture feeds into emotional eating by promoting restrictive eating patterns. These diets often come with lists of 'good' and 'bad' foods, creating anxiety around eating and setting us up for feelings of shame when we don't adhere strictly to these rules. This anxiety can lead to a cycle of restrictive eating, followed by inevitable binges when the restriction becomes too much to bear. The guilt from bingeing then leads back to restriction, creating a vicious cycle that can be hard to break. It's a pattern many of us know too well, a pattern that disrupts both our physical and emotional health.

When we're taught that certain foods are 'bad', and eating them can trigger an emotional response that is disproportionate to the act of eating itself. This response is not about the food but what the food represents in the lexicon of diet culture. The cake is not just a cake but a test of willpower; the pizza is not just a meal but a potential slip-up. This mindset can turn eating, a necessary and potentially joyful part of life, to be a source of stress and self-loathing.

Moreover, the idealized images of bodies we see in the media can exacerbate these feelings. We are constantly being bombarded with images of bodies that fit a particular mold can skew our perception of what is expected and desirable, leading to dissatisfaction with our own perfectly normal and healthy bodies. This dissatisfaction can fuel emotional eating as we turn to food for comfort, to numb feelings of inadequacy, or as a way of rebelling against unrealistic standards.

Building media literacy *(also refer to chapter 5.2)* is crucial in disentangling ourselves from these harmful messages. It involves critically engaging with media content and assessing the intentions behind the messages we receive. It's about asking ourselves who benefits from these messages — the answer, more often than not, is industries that profit from our insecurities, be it the diet industry, fashion industry, or even specific sectors of the health and wellness industry.

 A practical step toward building media literacy is consciously curating your media consumption. This means following a diverse range of bodies and voices on social media, choosing magazines or blogs promoting body positivity, and being wary of content perpetuating diet culture. By changing the messages we are exposed to, we can start to change the way we think about our bodies and food.

Ultimately, reducing the impact of diet culture on our emotional eating habits involves a shift toward a more *compassionate and inclusive* understanding of health and beauty — one that celebrates diversity and listens to the body's needs rather than punishing it for not fitting a specific 'norm'. It involves recognizing that our value does not decrease because of someone's inability to see our worth, nor does it increase because we match an arbitrary standard of beauty.

Food is not a moral issue. It's nourishment, pleasure, culture, and conviviality. By reclaiming this perspective, we can begin to heal our relationship with food and ourselves, finding joy in eating and respecting our bodies just as they are.

As you navigate through these complex landscapes of media messages and societal expectations, remember, the quiet act of choosing self-compassion *(more in chapter 7.5)* over self-judgment can be revolutionary. It's not just about changing eating habits but changing the way we see ourselves and our bodies in a world that constantly tells us we are not enough.

When we shift that perspective and genuinely believe that we are enough as we are, food regains its rightful place in our lives: a source of nourishment and joy, not a battleground of willpower or a barometer of worth.

Chapter 2
Identifying Your Emotional Triggers

"It's easier to prevent bad habits than to break them"
~ Benjamin Franklin

Have you had one of those days where everything seems to pile up — a missed deadline, a forgotten appointment, a small argument that feels like the last straw. Suddenly, you find yourself standing in front of an open fridge, looking for something — anything — that might make you feel better. Sounds familiar, right? It's not just about hunger or what you eat; it's about what's eating at you.

This chapter is about spotting those sneaky emotional triggers that lead us to the kitchen and learning strategies to cope with them before they take us down a path of mindless eating.

2.1 The Most Common Emotional Triggers and How to Spot Them

Catalog of Triggers

Emotional eating can be tricky to identify because it often feels like normal eating; but it is triggered by various emotions that drive us to eat when we're not actually hungry. Stress is a big one. It's so easy to relieve a little bit of pressure with your favorite snack. Then there's boredom; sometimes, eating seems like the only way to break the monotony. Sadness and loneliness can also lead us to comfort foods; ice cream after a breakup is a cliché. Recognizing these emotions and understanding how they influence your eating behaviors can help you regain control.

Here are examples of emotional triggers or stressors that may lead to emotional eating:

- **Anger**: Reacting to conflicts or arguments with others, feeling frustrated or irritated by circumstances or people, dealing with unresolved anger or resentment.

- **Anxiety:** Anxious about the uncertainty of the future, career prospects, housing, or relationships.

- **Boredom:** Having idle time with nothing stimulating or engaging to do, feeling uninspired or uninterested in daily activities, experiencing monotony or lack of excitement in life

- **Celebration**: Overindulging in food during holidays like Thanksgiving or Christmas, associating desserts and treats with rewards for accomplishments, overeating at parties, weddings, or celebrations due to the festive atmosphere.

- **Disappointment:** Facing setbacks or failures in personal or professional goals, not achieving desired outcomes or expectations, feeling let down by oneself or others.

- **Fatigue:** Experiencing physical exhaustion from work or daily responsibilities, feeling mentally drained or overwhelmed by ongoing tasks, coping with sleep deprivation or insomnia.

- **Financial Strain:** Worrying about bills, debts, or financial instability.

- **Health Concerns:** Dealing with illness, chronic pain, or a loved one's health issues.

- **Habit:** Turning to snacks while watching TV or movies as a routine, eating out of boredom during long commutes or breaks at work, using food as a coping mechanism without consciously addressing emotions.

- **Loneliness**: Living alone and lacking social interaction or companionship, missing loved ones or feeling disconnected from friends and family or experiencing a sense of isolation or solitude.

- **Parenting Challenges:** Balancing parenting responsibilities, dealing with behavioral issues, or feeling overwhelmed as a parent.

- **Relationship Conflict:** Arguments, misunderstandings, or tension with a partner, family member, or friend.

- **Sadness:** Dealing with grief or loss of a loved one, a breakup or relationship issues, feeling down or depressed due to personal challenges or setbacks.

- **Social Anxiety:** Feeling nervous, self-conscious, or uncomfortable in social situations.

- **Stress:** Can be caused by any of the triggers mentioned above, or from juggling multiple responsibilities and tasks. At work, it can come from pressure from deadlines, workload, or demanding bosses.

Each emotion tends to trigger cravings for specific types of food. For example, stress might have you reaching for salty snacks like chips or pretzels, while sadness might steer you toward that pint of ice cream. It's fascinating how our emotions connect with such specific cravings. By acknowledging and understanding these patterns, you can take proactive steps to preempt or manage your emotional eating.

Self-Observation Techniques

Getting to know your emotional triggers requires a bit of detective work. It starts with awareness. Try to pause before you eat and ask yourself, "What am I really feeling right now?" Are you eating because you're genuinely hungry, or is there an emotion you might be trying to feed? This can be tough at first, but like any skill, it gets easier with practice.

Keeping a simple emotional diary *(also refer to chapter 2.5)* can be incredibly revealing. Just jot down what you feel when you reach for food. You may notice patterns that hadn't been obvious before. For instance, you may discover that you always snack a lot when you have a meeting with a difficult client, or when you're exhausted.

Trigger Patterns and Food Choices

As you become more attuned to your emotions and the foods you gravitate toward, you'll start to notice patterns. For instance, do you find yourself craving something sweet every time you feel rejected or under appreciated? Do salty snacks become your go-to comfort when you're bored or feeling uninspired?

Recognizing these patterns is not about judging yourself; it's about understanding yourself better. This understanding will gradually empower you to align your eating habits more closely with your physical needs rather than your emotional responses.

Emotional Awareness Exercise

PRACTICE

Let's try a simple exercise together. Next time you feel the urge to eat, stop and take a deep breath. Ask yourself:

- "What's really going on?"

- "Did something specific happen today that might be affecting my mood?"

- "Am I eating to procrastinate or avoid doing something?"

- "Am I hungry, or is something else driving me to eat?"

- "Will eating right now help me solve a problem or just provide temporary relief?"

Remember to write down your feelings or talk it out with someone you trust. Sometimes, acknowledging your emotions can diminish their power, helping you make a more mindful decision about eating.

As you gain a deeper insight into your emotional triggers and the emotions they provoke, you are reclaiming your power. This journey is not about depriving yourself of the joy of eating — it's about ensuring that when you do eat, it's for the right reasons. This chapter is your first stride toward breaking free from the cycle of emotional eating. As you cultivate this awareness and implement the strategies *(refer to chapter 3.6)*, you'll find yourself making choices that nurture your emotional and physical well-being.

2.2 The Link Between Emotional Eating and Unmet Emotional Needs or Past Trauma

Sometimes, the hunger you experience isn't for food but something more profound, perhaps a need from your past that remains unfulfilled. Emotional eating often stems from unmet emotional needs or unresolved past traumas. It's as if your psyche is searching for nourishment, and in the absence of addressing these deep-seated feelings, it turns to food as a substitute.

This isn't about physical hunger; it's a profound yearning for emotional fulfillment — the kind that food can never truly satisfy.

Imagine emotional needs as plants in a garden. Just like plants need water and sunlight to thrive, your emotional needs require attention and care. When these needs such as love, security, or self-esteem are neglected, you might find yourself trying to compensate by 'watering' these needs with food. It's a temporary fix, like covering a cracked window with tape. It may hold for a while, but the crack is still there. Recognizing this can be a pivotal moment in transforming your connection to food.

To identify these unmet needs, reflect on moments when you turn to food for comfort. What emotions are you actually feeding? Is it loneliness, a longing for affection, or perhaps a buffer against anxiety and fear? Sometimes, these patterns stem from as far back as childhood. Food may be a reward or a way to soothe distress during your younger years, establishing a pattern that you carry unconsciously into adulthood.

Addressing these deep-seated emotional issues is crucial in overcoming emotional eating. It involves exploring your past, recognizing the sources of your emotional hunger, and understanding that while food can distract from the pain temporarily, it doesn't solve the underlying issues. This exploration can be intense and might stir up unmet emotions you've long kept at bay.

Here, the role of self-compassion becomes vital. Approach these revelations not with judgment but with kindness and understanding toward yourself. If the issues are significant, such as those stemming from severe trauma, it is advisable to seek professional help from a therapist to help with this healing process.

Healthy Alternatives for Meeting Emotional Needs

While understanding and addressing your emotional needs and past traumas is fundamental, replacing the temporary comfort of food with more fulfilling activities and connections can lead to a more balanced, happier life. The list of various non-food reliefs are listed in *chapter 3.6 (Quick Reference: Triggers and how to manage them)*.

Letting Go: A Path to Healing and Self-Discovery

'Letting Go' is a powerful method that isn't just a trendy buzzword; it's a tried-and-tested technique used in various therapeutic practices like mindfulness-based therapies, cognitive-behavioral therapy (CBT), and acceptance and commitment therapy (ACT). It's a transformative approach to managing unresolved emotions and past traumas; it's like having a secret key to unlock the chains of negativity and pave the way to emotional liberation.

The essence of the 'Letting Go' method lies in its profound simplicity. It's about releasing the tight grip we often have on negative emotions, thoughts, and past experiences that no longer serve us. Create a mental picture of shedding layers of emotional baggage, one by one, until you feel lighter, freer, and more in tune with your authentic self.

But let's be real; this journey isn't always a walk in the park. It requires patience, self-awareness, and a genuine willingness to dive deep into your emotional landscape. It's about facing the shadows within with courage and compassion, knowing that true healing comes from embracing our vulnerabilities.

By incorporating the 'Letting Go' strategy, you can cultivate greater emotional resilience, release past burdens, build emotional resilience, and well-being. It's a process of untangling old wounds, rewiring unhelpful thought patterns, and nurturing a positive relationship with yourself and food.

So, if you're ready to release the past burdens that weigh you down, cultivate inner peace, and create a brighter, more nourishing connection with yourself and your relationship with food, then the 'Letting Go' method is your guiding light on this transformative journey.

Guide To Letting Go

Here's a quick guide on using the 'Letting Go' method to overcome unresolved emotional issues and childhood traumas, related to emotional eating:

Acknowledge and Accept Emotions:

Begin by acknowledging and accepting your emotions, including any painful or uncomfortable feelings related to past experiences or trauma. Understand that it's normal to experience various emotions, and suppressing or avoiding them can contribute to emotional eating behaviors.

Mindful Awareness:

Practice mindfulness to cultivate present-moment awareness without judgment. Mindfulness techniques, such as meditation, or mindful breathing, can help you observe emotions and thoughts with curiosity and compassion. Bring mindful awareness to your eating habits, noticing any emotional triggers or patterns without self-criticism.

Identify Triggers and Patterns:

Explore the connections between past emotional experiences, childhood trauma, and your current emotional eating behaviors. Identify specific triggers, such as stress, anxiety, loneliness, or certain emotions, that lead to emotional eating episodes.

Emotional Processing:

Engage in emotional processing techniques to release pent-up emotions and address unresolved issues. This may involve journaling *(refer to chapter 2.5)*, expressive arts therapy, or talking to a therapist or trusted confidant. Allow yourself to express emotions in a safe and supportive environment, validating your experiences and promoting healing.

Practice Self-Compassion:

Cultivate self-compassion by treating yourself with love, care, kindness, understanding, and acceptance. Recognize that emotional eating behaviors often stem from underlying emotional pain or distress. Be gentle with yourself during the healing process, acknowledging that it's okay to feel vulnerable and seek support.

Letting Go Meditation:

Incorporate 'letting go' meditation practices into your routine. During these meditations, focus on releasing attachments to negative emotions, thoughts, and past traumas. Visualize yourself letting go of burdensome emotions, allowing them to dissolve and drift away as you cultivate a sense of inner peace and freedom.

Forgiveness and Healing:

Practice forgiveness, both towards yourself and others involved in past traumas or emotional wounds. Forgiveness doesn't mean condoning harmful actions but releasing resentment and finding closure. Explore forgiveness exercises, such as writing a forgiveness letter (even if not sent) or practicing loving-kindness meditation directed towards yourself and others.

Seek Professional Support:

Consider consulting with a counselor or therapist who specializes in trauma-informed care, mindfulness-based approaches, or emotional eating recovery. A therapist can provide further guidance, support, and techniques tailored to meet your specific needs and goals in overcoming unresolved emotional issues and trauma.

2.3 Food as Comfort: Why We Turn to Eating in Times of Emotional Turmoil

Isn't there something almost magical about how a particular food can transport us back to a moment of comfort? Whether it's the warm soup that reminds you of your grandmother's kitchen or the chocolate you reach for after a hard day's work, comfort food plays a substantial role in many of our lives. These foods often have a nostalgic or sentimental value linked to positive memories, providing an instant psychological comfort that goes beyond their nutritional value. The soothing effect of comfort food is real — it can trigger feel-good chemicals in the brain, similar to receiving a warm, loving hug.

As mentioned earlier, this is because eating those foods activates the release of dopamine, a neurotransmitter associated with feelings of pleasure and satisfaction. This response can be particularly strong when you're feeling low, stressed, or lonely, making these foods a quick fix to uplift your mood.

However, this psychological comfort can sometimes overshadow our actual nutritional needs. When you reach for cookies or chips as a way to cope with emotions, it's rarely about hunger. Instead, it's about trying to fill an emotional void with the quick satisfaction that these foods can provide. This can lead to a cycle where you're not addressing the underlying feelings but temporarily covering them up with comfort food. When you continue to feed your body with such non-nutritious foods, your physical health will soon be affected.

Case Studies: Finding Comfort Beyond Food

Let's look at some real-life inspirations. Take, for example, Sarah, a 42-year-old teacher who found herself frequently turning to ice cream to cope with stress and loneliness. After recognizing her pattern, Sarah started replacing her ice cream sessions with evening walks, slowly changing her response to emotional stress. These walks not only improved her physical health but also provided her with the mental space to reflect and decompress, effectively reducing her emotional reliance on food.

Then there's Michael, who used to dive into fast food after stressful work days. He decided to channel his stress into creativity by starting a DIY project at home. This not only diverted his immediate urge to turn to food but also gave him a lasting sense of accomplishment and a new way to unwind after tough days.

Through examples like Sarah and Michael, it becomes evident that while the comfort provided by food is immediate, it's fleeting and can often lead to feelings of guilt or dissatisfaction. Replacing this temporary comfort with activities that offer longer-lasting fulfillment can significantly alter our emotional well-being and our interaction with food. It shifts the narrative from eating as a way to suppress feelings to engaging in activities that genuinely process and manage those emotions.

As you consider these alternatives, remember that the goal isn't to deprive yourself of comfort food entirely but to create a healthier balance. It's about making room for both nourishment and enjoyment, recognizing the roles they play in our lives, and choosing how we respond to our emotional needs in ways that serve us better in the long run.

2.4 Stress, Anxiety, and Boredom: A Triad of Emotional Eating

Stress, anxiety, and boredom often form a challenging trio that can significantly influence our eating habits, leading us to turn to food for relief or distraction. Anxiety can feel like a constant buzz of unsettling noise in the background, stress can feel like a heavy burden on your shoulders, and boredom a dull, persistent ache for something to happen. Interestingly, while the emotional experiences differ, many of us respond to these feelings by reaching for something to eat, hoping to mute the discomfort, even if just for a moment.

Understanding the Triad

Let's break down how each part of this triad contributes to emotional eating. Stress often triggers eating as a form of rapid relief. It's like pressing a temporary 'pause' button on the stressor. The relief comes from the physiological response, where stress prompts your adrenal glands to produce cortisol, a stress hormone that increases appetite.

Anxiety relates closely to stress but tends to be more about anticipation of future worries than immediate stressors. It can cause an uneasy feeling, and many try to silence it with comfort foods that release neurotransmitters like serotonin, creating temporary feelings of relief and happiness. Boredom eating, on the other hand, is less about relief and more about seeking stimulation. Eating becomes an activity that fills the time, provides sensory input, and distracts from the monotony.

Mind-Body Connection

The physiological responses to stress and anxiety involve more than just emotional discomfort; they have real, physical effects that can lead to increased hunger and cravings. The release of cortisol not only triggers hunger but also can lead to cravings for sweet, fatty, or salty foods — these foods give a temporary boost in energy and mood. This is your body's way of preparing to either 'fight' or 'flight' from stressors by demanding quick energy, even though these situations rarely require a physical response. Recognizing this can change how you respond to stress and anxiety. Instead of turning to food, consider other ways to expend energy and regulate your mood, such as exercise or deep-breathing exercises.

Boredom as a Trigger

While stress and anxiety send us to the fridge in search of relief, boredom often sends us there in search of excitement. Boredom eating is usually mindless, where you might find yourself eating without really noticing what or how much you're consuming. It's not driven by hunger but by the desire to feel something different, to break the monotony. The key to combating boredom eating is engagement — keeping your mind occupied with tasks or activities that are stimulating and fulfilling. This could be anything from starting a new hobby, diving into a good book, or tackling a project you've been putting off.

Holistic Management Strategies

Addressing emotional eating caused by stress, anxiety, and boredom requires a holistic approach that considers both the mind and the body. It's about creating a life where there's less room for these feelings to drive you to the pantry. *Chapter 3.6* covers all the strategies you can adopt to manage these stressors. Additionally, establishing a routine will provide structure and reduce the unpredictability that often underlies stress and anxiety.

2.5 Using a Food and Mood Diary to Uncover Your Emotional Eating Patterns

A diary isn't just for recording daily events or your innermost thoughts. It can also be a powerful tool to decode your eating habits, especially when emotions drive your food choices. A detailed food and mood diary helps you track what you eat and records the circumstances and emotions surrounding each eating episode.

This practice can unearth patterns you might never have noticed — like reaching for a chocolate bar every time you feel unappreciated at work or indulging in fast food when you feel lonely on weekends.

The Role of Journaling

Journaling your food intake and associated emotions creates a map of your eating behavior, providing clear evidence of what triggers your emotional eating. Over time, you'll start to see patterns. Maybe you'll notice that anxiety leads you to snack continuously or that boredom has you visiting the fridge more often than you'd like to admit. This isn't about tracking calories or creating a diet chart — it's about understanding the link between your feelings and food, giving you insights into why you eat the way you do.

By documenting your meals and the emotions that accompany them, you can start to differentiate between eating out of hunger and eating driven by feelings. Sometimes, just the act of writing down what you're about to eat can make you stop and think, helping you make more conscious food choices. It's about becoming an observer of your own life, spotting trends, and recognizing triggers.

To help you get started with journaling, just scan this QR code or use the link below to download a digital copy of this Journaling Basics Guide: bit.ly/ee-journaling

Journaling Basics
How To Get Started

Starting a journal can be a rewarding way to reflect on your life, explore your feelings, and document your personal growth. Here's a simple guide to help you begin this enriching practice:

1. Choose Your Medium
Decide whether you prefer a traditional paper journal or a digital version. Paper journals (simple notebook) offer a tangible, personal touch and can be satisfying to write in, while digital journals are portable and often come with added features like password protection and search functionality.

2. Set Your Routine
Consistency helps turn journaling into a habit. Choose a time of day when you can sit down undisturbed. Whether it's in the morning to set your intentions for the day, or in the evening to reflect on what happened, find a time that suits your schedule and stick to it.

3. Create Your Comfortable Space
Make your journaling a ritual by creating a comfortable environment. This could be a quiet corner in your home with a cozy chair, good lighting, and perhaps a cup of your favorite tea or coffee.

4. Start With Simple Prompts
If you're unsure what to write about, start with simple (gratitude) prompts such as:
  - What are the three things I'm grateful for today?
  - What did I learn today?
  - How am I feeling right now, and why?
  - What are my goals for tomorrow?

5. Keep It Personal
Remember, your journal is a private space. Write openly and honestly. It's not about crafting perfect sentences—it's about expressing your true self.

6. Review Regularly
Every once in a while, take time to read back through your entries. This can help you see patterns in your thoughts and behavior, recognize your growth, and reflect on past experiences.

7. Be Patient With Yourself
Journaling is a personal process that evolves over time. Don't worry if you miss a day or two, or if you start by writing a few lines. What matters is that you return to it and continue to explore your thoughts and feelings.

By following these steps, you can begin journaling with confidence and curiosity, making it a valuable addition to your daily routine.

Emotional Eating by Kitty Barrett

How to Keep a Food and Mood Diary

Start by choosing a medium you're comfortable with, whether it is a digital app designed for food and mood tracking, or a simple physical notebook that will serve as your diary or journal. Every time you eat, jot down a few key details:

- What you ate: Write down everything you consume, no matter how small.

- How much you ate: Estimate portions to get a sense of quantity.

- When you ate: Note the time of day.

- Where you ate: Were you at your desk, in the car, or at the dining table?

- Who you were with: Were you dining alone, with colleagues, friends, or family?

- How you felt before eating: Were you angry, sad, stressed, bored, or happy?

- Your hunger level: Were you mildly hungry, starving, or not hungry at all?

Make this a habit for at least a few weeks. The more data you gather, the more patterns you can identify.

Analyzing Your Diary for Insights

After accumulating entries for some time, set aside a moment for analysis. Look for patterns and correlations between your emotions and eating habits. Do certain feelings like stress or sadness consistently lead to overeating or choosing unhealthy snacks? Are there specific times of day or social situations where you're more likely to eat emotionally?

This analysis can be eye-opening, revealing the emotional roots of your eating habits. It may feel overwhelming to see these patterns laid out, but remember, this is about gaining knowledge to foster change, not about self-judgment.

Actionable Steps Based on Insights

Armed with the insights from your diary, you can start to implement changes that help manage your emotional eating. *Refer to chapter 3.6: Triggers and Strategies.*

ACTION Plan for known triggers. If boredom is a frequent trigger, make a list of engaging activities you can turn to instead of food. Keep healthy snacks handy when you truly are hungry and need a quick bite. By preparing alternatives in advance, you reduce the likelihood of emotional eating.

This practice of journaling and analyzing isn't just about changing what or how you eat; it's about understanding and modifying the underlying emotional triggers that influence your eating habits. Doing this over time will lead to more mindful eating patterns and a healthier connection with food.

As we close this chapter, let's remind ourselves that the insights gained from keeping a food and mood diary are stepping stones to a deeper understanding of your feelings toward food. They connect to a larger picture of self-awareness and intentional living.

In the next chapter, we'll build on these foundations, exploring ways to cultivate resilience and manage stress without turning to food, ensuring your progress in emotional eating is both sustainable and enriching.

Chapter 3
Emotional Eating Strategies - How To Beat It

"Let go of your mind and then be mindful. Close your ears and listen."

~ Rumi

Picture this: You're sitting down with your favorite meal, the aroma tantalizing, colors vibrant, and just the sight of it makes your mouth water. But instead of diving in headfirst, you take a moment to pause. You truly see the food, smell its richness, and anticipate enjoying every single bite. This is the essence of mindful eating, and it's about understanding and applying the principles of mindful eating to transform how you relate with food in the most beautiful way.

In this chapter, we will outline practical strategies and quick guides that will equip you to manage and overcome emotional eating over the long term.

3.1 The Power of Mindful Eating

What Is Mindful Eating?

Mindful eating is about engaging all your senses to experience food more intensely without judgment. It's a practice rooted in mindfulness, a form of meditation that encourages you to bring awareness to the present moment. When applied to eating, it means noticing your food's colors, flavors, textures, and smells, chewing your food slowly, and being attuned to your body's hunger and fullness signals. It's about recognizing the difference between eating to satisfy physical hunger and eating driven by emotional needs.

The Benefits of Mindful Eating

Mindful eating is a powerful tool to differentiate and respond appropriately to emotional versus physical hunger. It involves fully engaging with your eating experience: savoring each bite, recognizing the flavors, and being aware of how the food makes you feel. By eating slowly and without distractions, you can ask yourself: "Am I eating because I'm hungry or trying to soothe an emotion?" If it's the comfort you seek, consider other ways to find it. Perhaps a walk, a hot bath, or a chat with a friend could also satisfy that need. By practicing mindful eating, you can make conscious choices about food, leading to a healthier and more enjoyable eating experience.

Embracing mindful eating can be truly transformative. Physically, it helps improve digestion since eating slower and chewing well makes it easier for your body to process food. It can also help with weight management, giving your body the time to recognize when it's full, reducing the likelihood of overeating. On an emotional level, mindful eating helps you break free from automatic eating behaviors, like munching chips while distracted by the TV, which can lead to mindless overeating. By paying attention to what and how you eat, you're more likely to make nourishing choices rather than reactive ones based on stress, boredom, or other emotions.

Getting Started with Mindful Eating

If you're new to this, start simple. Try this at your next meal: turn off all screens and sit at a table. Take a few deep breaths before you begin, and commit to experiencing this meal with all your senses. Look at your food, notice its smell, and take a small bite. Chew slowly, exploring the texture and flavor in your mouth. Think about the ingredients and the effort that went into preparing this dish. This is not about rigidly scrutinizing every meal but rather about starting to change your approach to eating, one meal at a time.

Reflective Journaling Prompt

You can add this to your *'Food and Mood'* diary or journal *(refer to chapter 2.5)* to enhance your understanding and practice of mindful eating.

PRACTICE

After each meal, take a minute to write down:

- What you ate, how or where you ate it?

- Did you enjoy the food?

- Did you feel rushed?

- How did you feel during and after the meal?

Reflecting on these questions will help you become more conscious of your eating habits and encourage you to make more mindful choices.

When integrating mindful eating into your life, you're not just changing how you eat; you're changing how you feel about food. It's no longer just 'fuel' or a fleeting comfort for emotional needs — it becomes an experience, a moment of enjoyment, and a way to nourish both body and mind. As you practice, you'll find that this awareness spills over into other areas of your life, allowing you to live more fully, more aware, and, yes, more joyously.

So, the next time you sit down to eat, remind yourself that it's not just about filling your stomach but about feeding your soul, savoring each moment, and truly experiencing the joy of eating.

3.2 Mindful Eating in Practice: Strategies for Everyday Meals

When you begin to integrate mindful eating into your daily routine, the transformation starts in the kitchen, where your meals come to life. Think of meal planning and preparation as a canvas where you paint your intentions for a healthier, more connected eating experience. This process isn't just about deciding what to eat; it's about creating a positive bond with food from the ground up.

Let's talk about how meal planning can become a mindful practice. It starts with the choices you make shopping for groceries because it is an excellent way to start connecting with your food. Try visiting a local farmers' market where you can engage with the growers. Learn about where your produce comes from and how it's grown. Such interactions can deepen your appreciation for the food you'll later prepare and eat.

STRATEGY When planning your meals, consider the nutritional balance and what foods bring you joy and satisfaction. Incorporate colors, textures, and flavors that make you excited about eating. This anticipation is a healthy, mindful approach to food that celebrates its diversity and the pleasure it can bring.

Now, moving on to the preparation of your meals. This is where mindfulness can really come to the forefront. As you prepare your ingredients, pay attention to each step of the process. Notice the color of the peppers as you slice them, the sizzle of the garlic in the pan, and the aroma of fresh herbs. Each of these elements is an invitation to be present and engaged. Cooking then becomes a meditative practice, not just a chore to rush through. You might find that this awareness adds a layer of satisfaction to your meal that goes beyond taste alone.

Mindful eating exercises can transform your eating moments into meditative experiences. One famous practice is the 'raisin exercise' from mindfulness-based stress reduction programs. Here's how you can do it: Take a raisin and spend a few minutes exploring it as if you've never seen one before. Notice its texture, color, and shape. Smell it, roll it between your fingers, and listen to the sounds it makes. When you finally eat it, take your time to really taste it, feeling the textures and flavors unfold. This exercise can reveal how much there is to experience in just one small piece of food. It teaches you to slow down and truly appreciate what you're eating, which can be applied to any meal.

Another playful yet effective technique is using your *non-dominant hand to eat*. This naturally slows you down and makes you more conscious of each bite, which can be particularly helpful if you tend to eat quickly. It disrupts the automatic hand-to-mouth flow, forcing you to pay more attention to your eating. This can lead to eating less and enjoying your food more because you're fully present for each bite rather than just mechanically moving through your meal.

Incorporating these mindful practices into your meal planning, preparation, and eating helps transform the way we treat food. It shifts eating from being a reactive, often mindless act to a deliberate, fulfilling experience that nourishes not just your body but also your soul.

Through mindfulness, you reconnect with the joy of eating and the nourishment it provides, making each meal a celebration of life and health. This is not about rigid dietary restrictions or moralizing food choices; it's about fostering a deep, appreciative connection with what you eat and why you eat it.

As you continue to practice these techniques, you'll likely find that they not only change how you eat but also how you approach life — more present, more conscious, and more appreciative of the simple pleasures it offers.

3.3 Relearning Hunger and Fullness Cues

Understanding your body's natural signals for hunger and fullness is like learning a new language. Initially, it may feel foreign, especially if you've spent years overriding these cues with emotional eating or strict dieting. But just like any language, with a bit of practice and patience, you can become fluent, and this fluency can transform your eating habits and your approach to food.

First, you need to really tune into your body's signals. Hunger isn't just a growling stomach; it can also manifest as fatigue, irritability, or a slight headache. These are signs that are often easily ignored or misinterpreted.

On the other hand, fullness isn't about feeling stuffed or bloated; it's a gentle signal from your body that you've had enough, a sense of contentment and satisfaction from the meal. To start tuning into these cues, try to rate your hunger on a scale from 1 to 10 before you eat.

- '1' could mean you're so hungry you could eat anything in sight
- '3' or '4' is when you should start eating, when you're hungry but not ravenous
- '6' or '7' is when you should stop, when you are satisfied but not stuffed
- '10' might mean you're so full you feel uncomfortable

Mindful Eating vs. Mindless Eating

Contrast this with mindless eating, which is driven by distraction or emotion rather than hunger. Mindless eating often leads to eating too quickly, choosing unhealthy foods, and overeating. It's eating that popcorn bucket at the movies before you even realize what you're doing. Mindful eating is when you slow down and savor each bite. It checks against this automatic behavior, allowing you to make conscious choices about how much and what you eat.

Identify Hunger and Fullness Levels

PRACTICE One effective way to reconnect with these signals is to pause mid-meal. This pause can help you make a conscious choice about whether to continue eating rather than just continuing out of momentum.

- About halfway through your meal, put down your utensils and assess how you feel.
- Are you still eating because you're truly still hungry, or are you just finishing what's on your plate?

Another helpful exercise is to experiment with portion sizes.

- If you're used to filling your plate to the brim, try serving yourself slightly less than you need.
- You can always go back for more if you're genuinely still hungry.

This practice can help recalibrate your understanding of how much food your body actually needs to feel satisfied.

Challenges and Solutions

One common challenge many face when relearning these cues is the delay between eating and feeling full, known as satiety delay. Your brain takes about 20 minutes to register the feeling of 'fullness' from the time you start eating. In today's fast-paced world, many of us eat too quickly, and we can consume a lot more than we need before our brain has a chance to tell us we're full.

To combat this, try slowing your eating by putting your cutlery down between bites. Then chew your food thoroughly and really savor the flavors in your mouth. Not only will this help with digestion, but it will also give your body time to catch up with your brain, reducing the chances of overeating.

Another issue might arise from years of conditioned habits, such as eating everything on your plate regardless of hunger levels, possibly a remnant from childhood. To shift this habit, remind yourself that it's okay to leave food on your plate. It can be helpful to start using smaller plates to reduce portion sizes without feeling deprived.

Also, consider if what you're feeling is a hunger for food or perhaps an emotional need. If it's comfort or stress relief you're seeking, food won't satisfy these needs in the long run. Finding healthier coping methods, like engaging in a hobby, taking a slow walk, or talking to a friend, can be much more fulfilling.

Reconnecting with your body's hunger and fullness cues is a gentle journey of rediscovery. It's about listening to and respecting your body's needs, not just following a set of diet rules. Remember, every meal is an opportunity to practice, learn, and grow in understanding your body's unique language of hunger and fullness. As you continue to explore and honor these signals, you'll find yourself enjoying your meals more and feeling better physically and emotionally.

3.4 Combining Mindfulness with Emotional Awareness for Lasting Change

Merging mindfulness with emotional awareness creates a robust framework that can genuinely transform how you manage emotions and, consequently, how you manage eating. This integration is crucial because while mindfulness teaches you to stay present and aware, emotional awareness deepens your understanding of why you feel what you feel and how to handle these emotions without resorting to food. Together, they empower you to navigate the complexities of emotional eating with more finesse and self-compassion.

When you practice mindfulness, you become an observer of your thoughts and feelings without being swept away by them. It's like watching clouds pass across the sky, acknowledging their presence but knowing they are temporary. This perspective is invaluable when dealing with emotional eating because it allows you to recognize an emotional urge to eat without immediately acting on it. Now, layer this with emotional awareness, which involves understanding the what and why behind your emotions. For instance, if you're feeling stressed, emotional awareness helps you pinpoint the source — be it an impending deadline or a personal conflict, allowing you to address this stressor directly rather than using food as a coping mechanism.

Strategies for Emotional Awareness

Developing greater emotional awareness can start with something as simple and profound as journaling. You can also use your Food Mood diary or journal *(mentioned in chapter 2.5)* where you can record events and your feelings about them can offer surprising insights into your emotional patterns. Over time, you might notice that certain situations or interactions consistently trigger stress or sadness, which in turn leads you to seek comfort in eating. With this awareness, you can develop healthier responses to these emotions.

Reflective meditation is another powerful tool. This practice involves sitting quietly at the end of the day and replaying events in your mind. Rather than analyzing or judging, the goal is to observe and understand your emotional reactions. This practice can be enlightening, showing you how your emotions fluctuate and intersect throughout the day and how these emotions influence your eating habits.

Mindfulness in Emotional Regulation

Mindfulness plays a pivotal role in emotional regulation by helping you maintain a moment-to-moment awareness of your feelings. When an intense emotion like anger or sadness arises, mindfulness encourages you to pause and acknowledge the emotion instead of automatically turning to food. Breathing techniques, a staple in mindfulness practice, can be particularly effective here. Deep, focused breathing has a physiological effect on your nervous system that helps calm the body and mind, making it easier to deal with challenging emotions.

Practicing mindfulness during less stressful times can also prepare you to handle intense emotions more effectively when they arise. Regular mindfulness practice strengthens the parts of the brain responsible for emotional regulation and reduces activity in the amygdala (a small almond-shaped area in the brain). It is associated with fear and emotional responses, which can lead to more balanced emotional reactions overall.

Mindfulness meditation is a powerful tool that you can use. This involves sitting quietly and paying attention to the sensations of breathing, your thoughts, sounds, or parts of the body. The objective is to bring your mind's attention to the present and to avoid drifting into concerns about the past or future. This practice can help you recognize the emotional and physiological triggers that lead to stress eating, giving you the insight needed to intercept these impulses and make healthier choices. Incorporating regular mindfulness into your routine can change the way your brain responds to stress and reduce the reliance on food for emotional relief.

PRACTICE Here's one way to help you break the cycle of stress eating that doesn't involve raiding the refrigerator. *Breathing exercises* are a great place to start and they helps slow the heartbeat and can lower or stabilize blood pressure, creating a feeling of calm and reducing stress.. Try this:

1. Pause and take a few deep breaths the next time you feel overwhelmed.

2. Take deep breaths slowly through your nose. Let your chest and lower belly rise as you fill your lungs.

3. Hold your breath for a moment, then exhale slowly through your mouth.

Creating a Personalized Plan

Crafting a personalized mindfulness and emotional awareness plan involves identifying your unique emotional triggers and the specific mindfulness and emotional awareness strategies that best address these. Start by mapping out the emotions that typically lead to emotional eating. Next, choose techniques from your mindfulness and emotional awareness toolkit that resonate with you — whether it's journaling, reflective meditation, or mindfulness exercises like mindful walking or eating.

Set realistic goals for incorporating these practices into your daily routine. You could start with five minutes of meditation each morning or journaling for a few minutes each night. The key is consistency, as the benefits of mindfulness and emotional awareness build over time. As you become more practiced in these techniques, your need to turn to food in response to emotions diminishes.

Integrating mindfulness with emotional awareness isn't just about improving how you eat; it's about enriching how you live. When you become more attuned to your inner experiences and learn to manage your emotions more effectively, you open the door to a more balanced, fulfilling life. As you continue to explore and apply these practices, let's not forget that each step forward, no matter how small, is a step toward a more mindful, emotionally intelligent you.

In this chapter, we've explored how intertwining mindfulness with emotional awareness can provide powerful tools to combat emotional eating and enhance your overall emotional well-being. We delved into practical strategies like journaling and reflective meditation that help foster emotional awareness, and we discussed how mindfulness can be a crucial player in regulating difficult emotions.

The journey to overcoming emotional eating is profoundly personal and constantly evolving. Each day offers a new chance to apply these practices, learn more about yourself, and continue making choices that support your health and happiness. In the next chapter, we'll expand on these concepts, exploring how to translate this newfound awareness and regulation into lasting lifestyle changes that support your goals.

3.5 The 4-Step S-T-O-P Method

In these two sub-chapters, we will go through the method and strategies of managing, and eventually, conquering emotional eating.

Managing emotional eating can feel like an uphill battle; but with this **4-step S-T-O-P method**, you'll be able to manage it in the long run. It consolidates all that was mentioned earlier into a simple process, as a guide and reminder, to help you overcome the emotional impulses that lead to unhealthy eating habits.

Let's remind ourselves of this process; here's the step-by-step guide to this S-T-O-P Method.

S: Spot the Trigger

Identify the Emotional Eating Triggers:

First step, we need to figure out what's setting off your cravings. Is it stress from work, boredom on a lazy afternoon, or that nagging feeling of loneliness?

Journal: Keep a daily log of emotions and situations that lead to cravings. Grab a journal and start jotting down the emotions and situations that make you want to reach for those comfort foods. Writing down your thoughts and feelings can help you see patterns over time. Note the time, place, and emotions when you feel the urge to eat. Being mindful and aware of these triggers is the crucial first step.

Awareness: Pay attention to specific times and events that make you want to eat. Be conscious of your emotions throughout the day. Are you stressed, bored, lonely, or anxious? Recognizing these emotions can help you understand your triggers.

Mindfulness: Practice mindfulness techniques to stay present and notice what you're feeling right before you reach for food. This helps you become more aware of your triggers in real-time and reduces impulsive reactions.

T: Think and Reflect

Recognize Your Eating Patterns:

Next, let's take a moment to pause and reflect. Recognizing whether your hunger is a physical need for food or an emotional state is crucial. It's all about taking that moment to think before you eat.

Pause: Before eating, take a moment to reflect on why you want to eat. Take a deep breath and pause for a few moments before you eat. This gives you time to think about your motivations.

Assess Hunger: Are you physically hungry or just eating to soothe emotions? When you suddenly feel the urge to snack, just stop and ask yourself, "Why do I need to snack?" Ask yourself if you're eating because you're hungry or if you're using food to deal with emotions. True hunger builds gradually, while emotional hunger often feels sudden and urgent.

Identify Patterns: Reflect on your eating patterns. Look for recurring themes or times when emotional eating happens most. Do you reach for snacks when you're stressed or bored? Understanding your patterns can help you address the root cause.

O: Opt for Alternatives

Use Sustainable Tools and Strategies:

Now, let's find some healthier ways to cope with those emotions. You can also refer to chapter 3.6: Triggers and Strategies.

Healthy Distractions: Instead of diving into a tub of ice cream, try engaging in activities that keep your mind off food and bring you joy.

Self-Soothing Techniques: Develop a toolkit of non-food self-soothing techniques. These could include deep breathing exercises, progressive muscle relaxation, meditation or listening to calming music.

Support System: Lean on your support network. Talking to friends, joining support groups, or seeking professional counseling can provide the emotional support you need without turning to food.

P: Plan and Prepare

Manage Emotional Eating Long-Term:

Finally, let's set you up for success. Planning your meals and snacks ahead of time can help you make healthier choices when emotions run high.

Meal Planning: Prepare healthy meals and snacks in advance to avoid impulsive eating. Plan your meals and snacks for the whole week. Having healthy options readily available can help reduce the temptation to grab unhealthy snacks when emotions run high.

Routine Building: Establish regular meal times and stick to them in order to help you stay on track. Consistency can help stabilize your eating habits and reduce emotional eating.

Mindful Eating: Practice mindful eating by slowing down your eating process to savor each bite, and paying attention to your hunger and fullness cues. Eat slowly and focus on the taste, texture, and satisfaction of your food. This will help you enjoy your meals better and recognize when you are full.

Embrace the Journey

Breaking the cycle of emotional eating is a journey, and it's okay to take it one step at a time. The S-T-O-P method is here to help you build awareness, make thoughtful choices, and create a healthier relationship with food. So next time you feel those cravings kicking in, just remember to S-T-O-P and take control of your emotional eating journey. You've got this!

3.6 How To Manage Emotional Eating

Strategies & Quick Guides

By understanding and addressing the different emotional triggers, you can develop strategies that minimize the impact of these emotions on your eating habits and enhance your overall well-being.

The key is to have a repertoire of activities that fulfill you emotionally and intellectually — without involving food. Food might offer a quick fix, but human connection provides more profound healing.

For your convenience, here is a quick reference guide of the strategies mentioned earlier, aimed at helping you effectively manage and overcome emotional eating sustainably.

Five Ways to Recognize Emotional Eating Patterns

RESOURCE The following can help you recognize emotional eating patterns and deepen your understanding of the underlying triggers, emotions, and behaviors associated with emotional eating. This awareness forms the basis for developing effective strategies to address and manage this eating behaviors.

1. Recognize Physical vs. Emotional Hunger:

- You will learn to distinguish between physical and emotional hunger. Physical hunger gradually builds up and is often located in the stomach. In contrast, emotional hunger can feel sudden and often makes you crave specific emotions like stress, boredom, or sadness.

- Before eating, pause and ask yourself if you're eating because your body needs nourishment or eating in response to an emotion.

2. Keep a Food Diary:

- Maintaining a food diary can help you track your eating patterns, emotions, and triggers. Record what you eat, when, how you feel before and after eating, and any events or emotions that may have influenced your food choices.

- Review your food diary regularly to identify patterns and associations between emotions and eating behaviors.

3. Identify Triggers and Associations:

- Pay attention to specific triggers that lead to emotional eating episodes. These triggers can be external (e.g., stressful situations, social gatherings, certain environments) or internal (e.g., specific emotions, thoughts, memories).

- Notice associations between certain emotions or situations and your urge to eat. For example, do you tend to reach for snacks when feeling anxious or bored?

4. motional Check-Ins:

- Practice regular emotional check-ins throughout the day to assess your emotional state. Use a journal or mood-tracking app to record your feelings, moods, and thoughts at different times.

- Look for patterns in your emotional check-ins and notice if there are specific emotions that consistently precede or accompany episodes of emotional eating.

5. Physical and Behavioral Signs:

- Pay attention to physical and behavioral signs that may indicate emotional eating. These signs can include eating quickly or mindlessly, continuing to eat despite feeling full, seeking out specific comfort foods, or feeling guilty or ashamed after eating.

- Notice any changes in your eating habits, such as eating at irregular times, eating in secret, or using food as a primary coping mechanism for emotions.

Once you've pinpointed your emotional triggers and the foods you typically crave, it's time to put strategies into action. We will cover the triggers and strategies in *chapter 3.6*.

Triggers & Strategies

Here's a helpful resource; it's a comprehensive approach to manage each specific emotional eating trigger. You can use this in conjunction with the **S-T-O-P Method** covered earlier.

Quick Reference: Typical 'go-to' comfort foods

These are the usual comfort foods; remember to be mindful each time you reach out to eat these foods when you are not actually hungry.

Spicy snacks, fast food, convenience foods, chocolate, ice cream, cookies, sweets, candy, sugary drinks, pastries, popcorn, candy, alcohol, energy drinks, desserts, rich meals, cake, chips, pizza, macaroni, pasta, cheese, caffeine, rich meals.

Quick Reference: Triggers and how to manage them

Anger:

- Identify situations triggering anger responses.
- Observe if anger leads to emotional eating or overeating behaviors.
- Practice deep breathing, engage in physical activity, journal emotions, seek anger management support, listen to calming music.

Anxiety:

- Keep a journal of anxiety- inducing situations.
- Notice if anxiety triggers mindless eating or specific food cravings.
- Practice mindfulness meditation, progressive muscle relaxation, seek professional support, use grounding techniques, and exercise regularly.

Body Image Dissatisfaction:

- Journal about body image thoughts and feelings.
- Identify if negative body image triggers restrictive eating behaviors.
- Practice body-positive affirmations, seek body image counseling, engage in enjoyable physical activities, follow body-positive social media, create a self-care routine.

Boredom:

- Track periods of boredom and idle time.

- Recognize if boredom leads to mindless snacking or food searching.
- Engage in hobbies, read a book, go for a walk, gardening, painting, practice mindfulness, try new activities, take up a craft or DIY project or even clearing out that neglected closet.

Confusion:

- Note situations causing confusion or uncertainty; track times of indecision or lack of clarity.
- Observe if confusion leads to emotional eating or seeking comfort foods.
- Practice mindfulness, clarify thoughts and decisions, seek professional guidance, create a pros and cons list, talk to a trusted friend.

Disappointment:

- Keep track of disappointments and letdowns.
- Recognize if disappointment leads to emotional eating or seeking treats.
- Practice self-compassion, focus on positive aspects, engage in uplifting activities, write about feelings, do a favorite activity.

Emotional Numbness:

- Reflect on times when emotions feel dulled or absent.
- Identify if emotional numbness triggers desire for comfort foods.
- Engage in sensory experiences, practice emotional awareness, seek therapy or counseling, connect with nature, listen to music.

Fatigue:

- Monitor periods of fatigue or exhaustion.
- Notice if fatigue leads to cravings for energy-dense or sugary foods.
- Prioritize sleep, rest, relaxation techniques, avoid stimulants close to bedtime, establish a bedtime routine, take short naps, reduce caffeine intake.

Fear:

- Reflect on situations causing fear or anxiety.
- Observe if fear leads to seeking comfort foods or overeating.
- Practice deep breathing, face fears gradually, seek professional help, talk to a friend, use relaxation techniques.

Financial Stress:

- Track financial stressors and worries.
- Recognize if financial stress affects food choices or leads to emotional eating.
- Budgeting, seeking financial advice, engaging in low-cost self-care activities, stress management techniques, and cooking at home.

Frustration:

- Track moments of frustration or irritation, keep a log and note triggers.
- Observe if frustration leads to emotional eating or cravings for specific foods.

- Practice relaxation techniques, communicate feelings, engage in enjoyable activities, do deep breathing exercises, take a break.

Habit:

- Identify habitual eating behaviors or routines.

- Recognize patterns of automatic or mindless eating based on habits, notice if eating happens automatically without hunger signals.

- Create new habits, practice mindful eating, break associations with food and routines, set specific meal times, replace snacks with healthy options, avoid multitasking while eating.

Happiness/Celebration:

- Record moments of joy and celebration.

- Notice if happiness triggers indulgence or overeating as a form of celebration.

- Practice moderation, celebrate with non-food rewards, enjoy experiences, share with others, focus on portion control, focus on experiences rather than food.

Insecurity:

- Reflect on situations that evoke feelings of insecurity or moments of self-doubt.

- Observe if insecurity leads to emotional eating or seeking comfort foods.

- Practice self-compassion, challenge negative thoughts, seek support from loved ones, build self-confidence, engage in self-care activities and positive self-talk.

Isolation:

- Track times of isolation or loneliness.
- Notice if isolation triggers emotional eating or cravings for company.
- Reach out to loved ones, engage in social activities, join groups or clubs, seek social support, and volunteer.

Loneliness:

- Note periods of loneliness or social disconnection.
- Identify if loneliness leads to emotional eating or seeking food for comfort.
- Connect with others, engage in social activities, seek emotional support, practice self-care, volunteer or adopt a pet.

Overwhelm:

- Journal situations that caused a sense of being overwhelmed.
- Recognize if overwhelm leads to emotional eating, overeating or specific cravings.
- Practice stress management techniques, break tasks into smaller steps, seek professional guidance, use to-do lists, delegate tasks, prioritize tasks, practice relaxation techniques.

Procrastination:

- Track instances of procrastination.
- Notice if procrastination leads to emotional eating or seeking distractions.

- Break tasks into smaller steps, create deadlines, practice time management, engage in enjoyable activities, use productivity tools.

Relationship Conflict:

- Journal about conflicts or disagreements.
- Observe if relationship conflict triggers emotional eating or comfort seeking.
- Practice effective communication, seek conflict resolution skills, engage in relationship counseling, take a walk to cool off, write a letter.

Sadness:

- Reflect on moments of sadness or emotional distress.
- Identify if sadness leads to emotional eating or cravings for comfort foods.
- Practice self-compassion, engage in uplifting activities, watch a comedy, take a warm bath or reach out to a friend or engage in social activities can be a great alternative to eating.

Social Pressure:

- Track situations involving social pressure.
- Notice if social pressure leads to emotional eating or indulgence.
- Practice assertiveness, set boundaries, seek supportive social circles, focus on personal values, and avoid peer pressure.

Stress:

- Keep a stress log and identify stressors.

- Recognize if stress leads to emotional eating or cravings for specific foods.

- Practice relaxation, meditation or breathing techniques, take up yoga, engage in physical activity but ensuring you're getting enough rest, or seek stress management support.

- You can download a digital copy of this quick reference list of emotional triggers - just scan this QR code or use the link below: https://bit.ly/ee-triggers1

Quick Reference ~ Emotional Triggers

TRIGGERS	HOW TO MANAGE THEM
Anger	<ul><li>Identify situations triggering anger responses.</li><li>Observe if anger leads to emotional eating or overeating behaviors.</li><li>Practice deep breathing, engage in physical activity, journal emotions, seek anger management support, listen to calming music.</li></ul>
Anxiety	<ul><li>Keep a journal of anxiety- inducing situations.</li><li>Notice if anxiety triggers mindless eating or specific food cravings.</li><li>Practice mindfulness meditation, progressive muscle relaxation, seek professional support, use grounding techniques, and exercise regularly.</li></ul>
Body Image Dissatisfaction	<ul><li>Journal about body image thoughts and feelings.</li><li>Identify if negative body image triggers restrictive eating behaviors.</li><li>Practice body-positive affirmations, seek body image counseling, engage in enjoyable physical activities, follow body-positive social media, create a self-care routine.</li></ul>
Boredom	<ul><li>Track periods of boredom and idle time.</li><li>Recognize if boredom leads to mindless snacking or food searching.</li><li>Engage in hobbies, read a book, go for a walk, gardening, painting, practice mindfulness, try new activities, take up a craft or DIY project or even clearing out that neglected closet.</li></ul>
Confusion	<ul><li>Note situations causing confusion or uncertainty; track times of indecision or lack of clarity.</li><li>Observe if confusion leads to emotional eating or seeking comfort foods.</li><li>Practice mindfulness, clarify thoughts and decisions, seek professional guidance, create a pros and cons list, talk to a trusted friend.</li></ul>
Disappointment	<ul><li>Keep track of disappointments and letdowns.</li><li>Recognize if disappointment leads to emotional eating or seeking treats.</li><li>Practice self-compassion, focus on positive aspects, engage in uplifting activities, write about feelings, do a favorite activity.</li></ul>
Emotional Numbness	<ul><li>Reflect on times when emotions feel dulled or absent.</li><li>Identify if emotional numbness triggers desire for comfort foods.</li><li>Engage in sensory experiences, practice emotional awareness, seek therapy or counseling, connect with nature, listen to music.</li></ul>
Fatigue	<ul><li>Monitor periods of fatigue or exhaustion.</li><li>Notice if fatigue leads to cravings for energy-dense or sugary foods.</li><li>Prioritize sleep, rest, relaxation techniques, avoid stimulants close to bedtime, establish a bedtime routine, take short naps, reduce caffeine intake.</li></ul>
Fear	<ul><li>Reflect on situations causing fear or anxiety.</li><li>Observe if fear leads to seeking comfort foods or overeating.</li><li>Practice deep breathing, face fears gradually, seek professional help, talk to a friend, use relaxation techniques.</li></ul>
Financial Stress	<ul><li>Track financial stressors and worries.</li><li>Recognize if financial stress affects food choices or leads to emotional eating.</li><li>Budgeting, seeking financial advice, engaging in low-cost self-care activities, stress management techniques, and cooking at home.</li></ul>
Frustration	<ul><li>Track moments of frustration or irritation, keep a log and note triggers.</li><li>Observe if frustration leads to emotional eating or cravings for specific foods.</li><li>Practice relaxation techniques, communicate feelings, engage in enjoyable activities, do deep breathing exercises, take a break.</li></ul>

Emotional Eating by Kitty Barrett

Quick Reference: More Empowering Activities to Help Conquer Emotional Eating

From mindfulness practices and stress-relief techniques to self-care rituals and creative outlets, these are examples of activities that you can engage in, to reclaim control over your relationship with food and emotions. It's all about finding what resonates with you and crafting a personalized toolkit for wellness and balance.

Aromatherapy:

Use essential oils or scented candles to create a calming atmosphere. Scents like lavender, peppermint, or citrus can promote relaxation, reduce anxiety, and improve mood respectively. Incorporate aromatherapy into your daily routine for emotional well-being.

Creative Outlets:

Express your emotions through creative outlets like drawing, painting, writing, or crafting. Creativity allows for self-expression, processing emotions, and finding healthy ways to cope with stress or negative feelings. Engage in creative activities regularly for emotional well-being.

Deep Breathing:

Practice deep breathing exercises to calm your mind and reduce stress. Take slow, deep breaths in through your nose and out through your mouth. Focus on the rhythm of your breath to promote relaxation and mindfulness.

Gardening:

Spend time caring for plants, gardening, or tending to a garden. Connecting with nature, nurturing living things, and engaging in physical activity outdoors can reduce stress, improve mood, and provide a sense of accomplishment. Incorporate gardening into your routine for mental and emotional health.

Mindful Eating:

Pay close attention to your food's taste, texture, and aroma. Eat slowly, chew thoroughly, and savor each bite. Focus on how the food makes you feel physically and emotionally. Avoid distractions like TV or phone during meals.

Hobbies:

Engage in activities you enjoy, such as painting, playing an instrument, or cooking healthy recipes. Hobbies offer a creative outlet, reduce stress, and provide a distraction from emotional eating triggers.

Hydration:

Drink a glass of water when you feel the urge to eat emotionally. Dehydration can sometimes be mistaken for hunger. Staying hydrated also supports overall health and digestion.

Journaling:

Write down your thoughts, emotions, and eating patterns in a journal. Track your triggers for emotional eating, such as stress or boredom. Reflect on your feelings before and after eating to gain insight into your relationship with food.

Listening to Music:

Play music that uplifts your mood or helps you relax. Music has a powerful impact on emotions and can serve as a distraction from emotional eating cues. Create playlists that resonate with your feelings and goals.

Meditation:

Set aside time for meditation to center yourself and quiet your mind. Focus on your breath or use guided meditation apps for support. Meditation can help reduce anxiety, increase self-awareness, and improve emotional regulation.

Mindful Breathing:

Practice mindful breathing exercises to ground yourself in the present moment. Focus on your breath, inhaling and exhaling slowly and deeply. Mindful breathing promotes relaxation, clarity of mind, and awareness of your emotions without judgment. Use it as a tool to manage stress and emotional triggers.

Nature Walks:

Take regular walks in nature to connect with the outdoors and boost your mood. Nature walks reduce stress, improve mental clarity, and provide a peaceful environment for reflection and relaxation. Incorporate nature walks into your routine for emotional well-being and mindfulness.

Physical Activity:

Engage in regular physical activity like jogging, dancing, or cycling. Exercise releases endorphins, which can improve mood and reduce stress. Find activities you enjoy to make exercise a positive part of your routine.

Playing with Pets:

Spend quality time with pets for companionship, comfort, and emotional support. Interacting with pets can reduce stress hormones, increase feelings of happiness, and provide a distraction from emotional eating cues. Enjoy playful activities with your pets to improve overall well-being.

Practicing Gratitude:

Take time each day to list things you're grateful for. Practicing gratitude shifts your focus to positive aspects of life and promotes a mindset of abundance and contentment. Express gratitude for your body and its abilities, fostering self-compassion and appreciation.

Progressive Muscle Relaxation:

Practice progressive muscle relaxation by tensing and then slowly releasing different muscle groups in your body. This technique reduces physical tension, relieves stress, and promotes relaxation. Use it regularly to unwind and manage emotional eating triggers.

Reading:

Escape into a good book or articles that interest you. Reading can shift your focus away from food, stimulate your mind, and provide relaxation. Choose reading material that inspires positivity and personal growth.

Taking a Bath:

Take a warm bath to relax your muscles and soothe your mind. Add calming scents like lavender or chamomile to enhance relaxation. Use bath time as a self-care ritual to unwind and reduce stress levels.

Talking to a Friend:

Reach out to a trusted friend or family member to talk about your emotions. Share your feelings, worries, and challenges related to emotional eating. Talking can provide support, perspective, and help you feel less isolated.

Volunteering:

Contribute your time and energy to volunteer work or helping others in need. Volunteering fosters a sense of purpose, connection, and gratitude. It shifts focus from personal concerns to making a positive impact, reducing the likelihood of emotional eating as a coping mechanism.

As we conclude this chapter on how to manage emotional eating, remember that the journey to understanding and overcoming your triggers is both deeply personal and profoundly transformative. The strategies we've explored are starting points to help you regain control and find healthier ways to cope with emotions.

Practice patience and persistence as you apply these techniques, and be kind to yourself along the way. Each step you take is a move towards a healthier relationship with food and, more importantly, with yourself. Remember, healing is not linear but a path marked by small victories and inevitable setbacks, each teaching you more about your resilience and strength.

Chapter 4
Transforming Your Relationship with Food

"Self-care is how you take your power back."

~ Lalah Delia

Imagine sitting down to a meal where each bite is a celebration, a moment of joy, free from guilt or regret. Where food is not an enemy or a source of anxiety but a delightful, nourishing presence in your life. This vision isn't just a far-off dream; it's within your reach. In this chapter, we will learn how to make peace with the plate before us and embrace a way of eating that enriches our lives rather than complicating them.

4.1 How to Enjoy All Foods Without Guilt or Bingeing

One of the most liberating things you can do is to give yourself unconditional permission to enjoy food. Yes, all foods. This might sound counterintuitive, especially if you've spent years trapped in a cycle of dieting, restriction, and guilt. But here's the thing: when you allow yourself to enjoy food without guilt, you actually empower yourself to make choices out of self-care rather than compulsion.

Permission to Enjoy

Giving yourself permission to enjoy food is about breaking down the mental barriers and food rules that diet culture has built. It's about stopping the labeling of foods as 'good' or 'bad'. Instead, seeing them simply as food, each type offering its own flavors and textures. This shift in perspective can reduce the anxiety and obsession around eating, making meals a more relaxed, enjoyable experience. When you stop viewing certain foods as forbidden, they lose their power over you. The chocolate that once seemed like a forbidden fruit, calling your name from the depths of your pantry, becomes just a sweet treat you can enjoy and then move on without bingeing.

Breaking the Cycle of Restriction and Bingeing

The cycle of restriction and bingeing is one of the most common patterns in emotional eating. It starts with restricting food, which inevitably leads to feelings of deprivation. And what happens when humans feel deprived? We want what we can't have even more. This often results in bingeing, followed by guilt, and then the cycle starts all over with more restriction.

Breaking this cycle involves practicing moderation, a key concept in mindful eating. It means allowing yourself to have a slice of cake at a party or a few pieces of candy from the office bowl, enjoying them thoroughly, and then simply continuing your day. Moderation allows you to enjoy all foods without overindulgence, and regain your control.

Coping with Guilt

Guilt after eating is like an uninvited dinner guest who ruins the party and it's crucial to address this. Start by challenging the guilt-inducing thoughts. If you catch yourself thinking, "I shouldn't have eaten that," try countering with, "Why not? It's perfectly okay to enjoy all kinds of food." Sometimes, just acknowledging these thoughts out loud can diminish their power.

Another effective strategy is to redirect your focus from guilt to gratitude. Instead of beating yourself up for what you ate, shift your attention to something positive about the meal, like how delicious or lovely it was to share with a friend. This reframing can help you build a healthier, more positive relationship with eating.

Journaling Prompt

ACTION To help you solidify these new habits, here's a journaling prompt: The next time you eat something you typically feel guilty about, take a moment afterward to jot down your feelings. Write about:

- Why did I choose to eat this food?
- What did I enjoy about it?
- How do I feel now?

To help you understand and reshape your relationship with food, try reflecting on these experiences — it reinforces the idea that it's okay to find pleasure in eating.

By embracing the joy of eating all foods without guilt, practicing moderation, and learning to cope with guilt constructively, you can transform how you feel about food, from anxiety and restriction to enjoyment and nourishment. This shift not only enhances your eating experiences but also contributes to a more balanced, fulfilling life where food is a source of pleasure and health, not a cause of stress.

4.2 Intuitive Eating: Listening to Your Body's Needs

Intuitive eating is like turning the volume up on your body's signals and turning down the noise from diet culture that clouds your feelings about food. It's about shifting from external rules about what, when, and how much to eat to trusting your body's cues.

It also enhances your eating experience, in a way that feels good and satisfying without counting calories or feeling guilty. This approach is built on ten core principles, each designed to support balanced, respectful, and health-focused eating behaviors.

Let's explore these principles, starting with the most fundamental one: rejecting the diet mentality. The diet mentality is the idea that there's a specific diet out there that will finally answer all your weight concerns. This mentality often leads to a cycle of yo-yo dieting, temporary weight loss followed by regaining, and a lot of frustration and guilt.

To truly adopt intuitive eating, it's vital to discard the mindset perpetuated by magazine articles and diet books that give false hope of losing weight quickly, easily, and permanently. It's about making peace with the fact that diets don't work long-term and trusting that your body knows best.

The second principle, perhaps one of the most liberating, is honoring your hunger. To prevent overeating, you must keep your body nutritionally fed with adequate energy and carbohydrates. When you let yourself become excessively hungry, you would lose all intentions of conscious and moderate eating.

Honoring this first biological signal sets the stage for rebuilding trust with yourself and food. Listen to your body signals, and eat something nourishing when you first begin to feel hungry. This might seem simple, but it requires tuning in to your body's cues and responding appropriately rather than ignoring them until you're ravenous.

Moving on, let's talk about discovering satiety, the principle that focuses on the experience of fullness. Understanding when you've had enough to eat is just as important as recognizing when you're hungry. It involves giving yourself the chance to recognize how the food makes you feel and the point at which you feel comfortably full. Satiety is a crucial part of eating because it allows you to live in balance with food. It's about stopping when you feel satisfied and comfortable, not stuffed or still hungry.

Try eating slowly to practice this, as it can take a few minutes for your brain to register that you're full. Pay attention to the taste of each bite, and notice how your satisfaction changes throughout the course of a meal.

Lastly, let's delve into the satisfaction factor, a principle often overlooked in traditional diets. The Japanese use wisdom to promote pleasure as one of their goals of healthy living, and it's a central theme in intuitive eating, too. Indulging in your favorite foods in a welcoming setting can create a profound sense of satisfaction and contentment due to the pleasure it brings.

When you create such an experience for yourself, you'll notice that it takes much less food to decide you've had 'enough'. Think about the last time you ate something just because it was available, even though you didn't really enjoy it. How satisfying was that experience? Now, imagine choosing to eat something because it's exactly what you feel like having. Notice the difference?

Embracing these principles of intuitive eating can transform your eating habits from rule-based to self-care-based. It's about making choices around food that feel good to your body without experiencing guilt or an obligation to eat a certain way.

This approach fosters a healthier approach to eating, one that's based on your body's natural needs and your personal satisfaction rather than external diet rules or societal trends. As you apply these principles, you likely find a significant shift in how you eat and feel about food and yourself.

4.3 The Importance of Nutritional Balance and Variety

When we talk about eating well, the terms 'balance' and 'variety' often come up, and there's a good reason. Picture your diet as a vibrant palette of colors, with each food group and type contributing a different shade. Just as a painter blends colors to create a masterpiece, blending various foods can create a nutritional masterpiece in your body.

This isn't about adhering to strict dietary rules that often lead to feelings of deprivation and subsequent binge eating. Instead, it's about understanding the principles of balanced eating that emphasize enjoying a wide range of foods, which can enhance both your physical health and emotional well-being.

Balanced eating is about ensuring your body gets the nutrients needed to function optimally. This means incorporating a mix of carbohydrates, proteins, fats, vitamins, and minerals into your diet. Carbohydrates, often demonized in diet culture, are actually your body's primary energy source. Whole grains, fruits, and vegetables not only provide energy but also contain fiber, which aids digestion and can help you feel full and satisfied.

Proteins play a crucial role in the building and repairing of tissues and can be found in animal products like meat and fish, as well as plant-based sources like beans and lentils. Fats, too, are essential, supporting cell growth, protecting your organs, and helping absorb nutrients. Choosing healthy fats like the ones in avocados, nuts, and olive oil can promote heart health and enhance overall vitality.

The beauty of embracing variety in your diet extends beyond mere nutrition; it also plays a significant role in your emotional relationship with food. When you allow yourself to enjoy a wide array of foods, you're less likely to feel restricted and more likely to feel satisfied with your meals.

This satisfaction is vital in preventing feelings of deprivation that can lead to emotional eating.

Additionally, exploring different foods can be a joyful, sensory experience. Think about the crunch of a fresh apple, the tang of a ripe tomato, or the creaminess of a well-made hummus. Each food brings its own unique flavor, texture, and pleasure, contributing to a more enjoyable and emotionally fulfilling eating experience.

Moreover, incorporating a variety of foods into your diet enhances your overall eating experience by ensuring that meals are not just nutritionally balanced but also interesting and enjoyable. Visualize sitting down to a meal with a colorful salad, a hearty piece of grilled fish, a side of aromatic brown rice, and a slice of juicy watermelon for dessert. This meal is not only pleasing to the eye but also provides a range of textures and flavors that stimulate the senses and make eating a pleasure rather than a chore.

Practice balanced eating

ACTION This simple visual guide can help ensure your meals are balanced and provide a good mix of macronutrients. Additionally, include a source of healthy fats in your meals, be it a drizzle of olive oil over your salad or a handful of nuts for a snack.

1. Focus on creating meals that include multiple food groups. Start by filling half your plate with vegetables and fruits: aim for a variety of colors to maximize the range of nutrients.

2. Allocate lean proteins and whole grains for each of the other two-quarters of the plate.

Embracing the principle of balance and variety in your diet is about more than just eating different foods; it's about establishing a harmonious connection with food that nurtures both your physical and emotional well-being. By embracing various nutritious foods, you'll satisfy your taste buds, nourish your body, and sidestep the drawbacks of restrictive eating habits, which can cause diet fatigue and emotional eating.

So, next time you plan a meal, think of it as a blank canvas to paint with the vibrant colors of fruits, vegetables, grains, proteins, and fats, creating a nutritional masterpiece that nourishes your body and soul.

4.4 Healthy Eating Hacks: Mind Over Meals

Let's be honest, sticking to healthy eating habits can be quite challenging. With all the tempting treats and busy schedules, it's easy to fall back into less-than-ideal eating habits. But guess what? You don't have to overhaul your entire life to start eating better. Sometimes, all it takes are a few clever mind tricks to help you make healthier choices without even realizing it.

In this section, you'll find some fun and simple mind tricks that can make a big difference in the way you manage your food intake. These strategies can help you steer towards healthier options, manage cravings, and enjoy your meals without the guilt more easily. Think of them as little hacks to outsmart your brain and support your journey to a healthier you.

1. ***Mindful portion control:*** To give the illusion of a fuller portion, use smaller plates and bowls, which can help reduce portion sizes without feeling deprived.

2. ***Prep healthy snacks:*** To encourage healthier snacking habits, keep nutritious snacks like cut fruits, veggies, nuts, or yogurt readily available and visible in your kitchen or workspace.

3. ***Colorful plate strategy:*** Make your meals visually appealing and nutritionally diverse by incorporating a variety of colorful vegetables and fruits.

4. ***Slow down while eating:*** Take your time to savor each bite, chew slowly, and put your utensils down between bites. This

mindful eating practice can help you enjoy your food more and recognize when you're comfortably full.

5. ***Hydration first:*** Drink a glass of water before meals to help control hunger cues and prevent overeating. Sometimes, thirst can be mistaken for hunger.

6. ***Healthy swaps:*** Replace unhealthy food items with healthier alternatives. Instead of using sour cream, why not use Greek yogurt instead? Or avocado instead of mayonnaise, or whole-grain bread instead of white bread?

7. ***Planning:*** Avoid impulsive and emotional eating – instead, plan your meals and snacks in advance. A meal plan can help you make healthier choices and stick to your nutritional goals.

8. ***Mindful indulgence:*** Allow yourself occasional treats in moderation without guilt. Savor these indulgences mindfully, focusing on taste and enjoyment rather than consuming them impulsively.

9. ***Keep a food journal:*** Track your food intake, emotions, and triggers in a journal to become more aware of your eating patterns and emotions surrounding food. This exercise will improve your self-awareness, enabling you to make informed food choices and identify areas for improvement.

10. ***Practice self-compassion:*** Be kind to yourself and avoid harsh self-criticism if you have setbacks or slip-ups. Learn to celebrate small victories and acknowledge your progress rather than focusing on perfection.

4.5 Replacing Emotional Eating Habits with Nourishing Practices

When life throws curveballs, as it often does, it's natural to seek comfort where it's easiest to find — and usually, that's food. However, replacing emotional eating with nourishing practices can transform how you eat and how you cope with life's ups and downs. The key is to find nourishing alternatives that fulfill not just your body but also your mind and soul.

Nutritional Guidance

In this section, we'll explore a few practical tips for making healthier food choices that can help you manage those pesky cravings. We'll talk about how balanced meals, mindful eating, and smart snacking can all play a role in overcoming emotional eating. Think of it as your friendly guide to nourishing your body and mind, helping you to stay positive throughout this journey.

Focus on Balanced Meals:

Your meal should include a variety of nutrient-rich foods such as lean proteins, healthy fats, fruits, vegetables and whole grains.Incorporate a rainbow of colorful fruits and vegetables to ensure a diverse intake of vitamins, minerals, and antioxidants.

Mindful Eating Practices:

Practice mindful eating by slowing down during meals, taking time to chew food thoroughly, and be aware of hunger and fullness cues. Avoid distractions like screens or multitasking while eating, allowing yourself to fully enjoy and savor your food.

Regular Eating Schedule:

Establish regular and consistent meal times to help regulate hunger hormones and prevent extreme hunger or overeating. Include balanced snacks if needed to maintain energy levels and prevent excessive hunger between meals.

Hydration:

Drink plenty of water to keep our body hydrated throughout the day. Quite often, thirst can be mistaken for hunger, so staying adequately hydrated can help prevent unnecessary snacking.

Avoid Restrictive Diets:

Avoid overly restrictive diets or extreme calorie counting, as they can add to feelings of deprivation that can lead to emotional eating episodes. Focus on nourishing your body with nutritious, satisfying foods rather than labeling foods as "good" or "bad."

Mindful Indulgences:

Allow yourself to enjoy occasional treats or indulgent foods in moderation without guilt. Practice mindful indulgence by savoring these foods and being present in the moment. Balance indulgences with nutritious meals and snacks to maintain overall dietary balance.

Nutrient-Dense Snacking:

Choose nutrient-dense snacks such as Greek yogurt with berries, a handful of nuts, whole-grain crackers with hummus, or sliced vegetables with guacamole. Include snacks that provide a combination of fiber, protein, and healthy fats to help you feel satisfied between meals.

Emotional Eating Alternatives:

Develop alternative strategies for managing emotions without turning to food. Engage in activities like journaling, talking to a friend, practicing relaxation techniques, or going for a walk. Identify and address emotional triggers rather than using food as a primary source of comfort or distraction.

Nutritional Education:

Seek out reliable sources of nutritional education and guidance to learn about balanced eating, portion control, and making healthier food choices. Work with a registered dietitian or nutritionist if needed to create a personalized nutrition plan that supports your emotional and physical well-being.

Self-Compassion and Flexibility:

Practice self-compassion and kindness toward yourself on your journey to recovery. Acknowledge that setbacks may occur, and focus on progress rather than perfection. Maintain flexibility in your eating habits and allow occasional deviations without judgment or guilt.

Identifying Nourishing Alternatives

STRATEGY Let's start by identifying practices that can serve as alternatives to reaching for that comforting snack. Consider activities that positively engage your senses and emotions. This could be anything from a soothing bath with essential oils to a brisk walk in a nearby park. It could be a creative outlet like painting, journaling, or practicing yoga or meditation. The idea is to create a list of go-to activities you can turn to when you feel the urge to eat due to stress, sadness, or boredom.

These should be activities that not only distract you from mindless eating but also enrich your life and bring you genuine joy and relaxation. You can add this list into your journal for quick reference.

Consider this:

- When you're feeling lonely or anxious and tend to snack, try scheduling regular coffee dates with friends or joining local clubs that match your interests. This addresses your emotional needs and builds your social network, providing a double dose of nourishment for your emotional well-being.

- If stress tends to be your trigger, engaging in regular physical activity can prove highly effective. This doesn't need to be intense exercise; even gentle movements like stretching or casual walking can significantly elevate your mood and reduce stress levels.

The Role of Mindful Eating in Nourishment

As discussed earlier in chapter 3, mindful eating is a powerful tool that can help reinforce your nourishment practices. It involves being fully present during meals, savoring each bite, and being attentive to how food affects your body and mood. This practice encourages you to choose foods not just for taste or habit but for how they nourish your body and contribute to your overall well-being.

For example, instead of hastily eating a salad because it's 'healthy', mindful eating encourages you to notice the freshness of the greens, the sweetness of the tomatoes, and the crunch of the nuts, all of which enhance your eating experience. This heightened awareness can transform eating from a mindless act to a joyful event that you look forward to because it satisfies more than just your hunger — it nourishes your spirit and your body.

Building a Support System

Finally, building a supportive social and environmental system is essential in sustaining these nourishing practices. Surround yourself with people who understand and support your goals, whether they are family members, friends, or support group members. These people will encourage you not just in your moments of success but also in times of struggle.

In addition to fostering supportive relationships, create an environment that reinforces your new habits. This might mean stocking your kitchen with foods that nourish you and make you feel good or setting up a cozy corner in your home where you can read, meditate, or practice yoga. Make your environment a sanctuary that supports your journey toward replacing emotional eating with truly nourishing practices.

Developing a Self-Care Routine

Developing a *self-care routine (also refer to chapter 5.4)* is crucial in ensuring these nourishing practices become a natural part of your life. A good self-care routine addresses your physical, emotional, and social needs, helping to maintain balance and prevent emotional eating triggers. Start by setting realistic goals for incorporating activities into your routine.

You could start your day with a 10-minute meditation to clear your mind or end your day by writing in a gratitude journal *(refer to chapter 4.5)*. Include regular physical activity that you enjoy, which could be anything from dancing to a fitness class to gardening.

It's also important to pay attention to your sleeping habits and to ensure that you get enough rest, as fatigue can often lead to emotional eating. Try creating a relaxing bedtime routine that may include reading a book or listening to soothing music, helping you wind down and improving your sleep quality. Remember, the goal of these routines isn't to fill your day with more tasks but rather to create spaces that help you live fully and healthily.

Weekly Mindful Self-Care Practice Plan

To create your own self-care plan, simply jot down one preferred activity you'd like to do in the morning, afternoon, and evening for each day of the week.

Scan this QR code or use the link below to download a digital copy of this chart: bit.ly/ee-selfcare1

By identifying nourishing alternatives, developing a comprehensive self-care routine, practicing mindful eating, and building a supportive network, you can foster a healthier bond with food and yourself. These steps are not just about avoiding emotional eating; they're about creating a fulfilling and joyful life where food is just one of many sources of pleasure and nourishment.

Weekly Mindful Self Care Practice Plan

DAY	MORNING	AFTERNOON	EVENING
Monday			
Tuesday			
Wednesday			
Thursday			
Friday			
Saturday			
Sunday			

DAY	MORNING	AFTERNOON	EVENING
Monday			
Tuesday			
Wednesday			
Thursday			
Friday			
Saturday			
Sunday			

4.6 Celebrating Food: Creating New, Positive Food Memories

In this chapter, we'll reconsider our perspective of food and transform it into a vibrant celebration of life. Food isn't just fuel; it can be a joyful celebration, a cultural journey, and a social connector that brings us together with others. By reframing the role of food in our lives, we can shift our focus from calorie counts and dietary restrictions to the joy and nourishment food brings. This shift can lead to healthier eating attitudes and profoundly enrich our lives.

Reframing the Role of Food in Life

Imagine seeing food as a delightful guest at your life's party rather than a foe that you must watch carefully or keep at bay. Food is not just nourishment, but also pleasure, tradition, and art. It's a homemade batch of your grandmother's cookies that brings back warm memories or the comforting aroma of a stew that simmers on the stove, filling the house with its scent.

When we start to see food this way, each meal becomes a learning opportunity to nourish our bodies, spirits, and connections with others. This perspective can liberate us from the cycle of guilt and restriction and lead us to a healthier relationship with eating.

Creating Positive Food Experiences

Positive food experiences can be powerful as they can transform eating from a mundane task into a meaningful and enjoyable event. Consider hosting a potluck where each friend brings a dish that holds special meaning or a family recipe.

This creates a meal and a tapestry of stories and traditions shared over plates of lovingly prepared food. Or perhaps, embrace the changing seasons with meals that highlight seasonal produce, celebrating the diversity and bounty of what each time of year brings. A summer barbecue with fresh corn and watermelon or a winter feast featuring hearty squashes and warm spices can be a delightful way to connect with the rhythm of nature and create lasting memories.

Another enriching experience can be cooking with others. Sharing the kitchen with family or friends isn't just about dividing tasks — it's about building bonds. Creating something delicious together can be a joyful and intimate experience, often punctuated with laughter, storytelling, and maybe a little mess.

It's about learning from each other, whether it's a new cooking technique or stories from a grandmother's kitchen. These moments allow food to become a bridge between generations and cultures, enriching your life far beyond the meal itself.

The Importance of Gratitude

Gratitude transforms how we approach life, and it can specifically alter our attitude toward food. Taking a moment before eating to express our thankfulness for the meal isn't just a ritual; it can enhance our eating experience by *grounding (more in chapter 7.2)* us in the moment and helping us appreciate the food in front of us.

Think about the journey the ingredients took to reach your plate: the sunshine, water, and care that made them grow, the hands that harvested them, and the work that went into preparing the dish. This mindful acknowledgment can deepen your appreciation for each bite, making the meal more satisfying and enjoyable.

Gratitude also extends to those who share your table. Acknowledging the pleasure of their company can make meals a cherished time for connection and sharing. It turns dinners into more than just eating; they become gatherings that feed your need for community and belonging. In this light, food is much more than sustenance; it's a catalyst for thankfulness, connection, and joy.

As you embrace these new frames of celebrating food, you create positive, vibrant food memories that can last a lifetime. These practices not only enhance your own life but also have the potential to influence those around you, spreading a positive and healthy approach to eating to your community. They allow you to celebrate life's moments, big and small, turning everyday meals into occasions of joy and gratitude.

To conclude this chapter, keep in mind that every meal presents a fresh chance to revel in the diverse tapestry of life, with all its flavors and stories. In the next chapter, we will explore how these celebrations can be woven into a sustainable lifestyle that helps support your long-term health and happiness, continuing to enrich your journey with food in ways that nourish both body and soul.

Chapter 5
The Role of Body Image in Emotional Eating

"You yourself, as much as anybody in the entire universe, deserve your love and affection."

~ Buddha

Have you ever caught yourself looking into a mirror, scrutinizing every inch of your reflection, yearning to change parts of your body? Or have you skipped a meal or two, hoping to conform to the unrealistic beauty standards set by glossy magazine covers and perfect Instagram feeds? If these situations resonate with you, rest assured, there are others who share similar experiences.

The connection between body image and our eating habits is not just a passing concern, but a deeply rooted issue in our society, often complicated by the overpowering influence of societal norms and media portrayals.

This chapter will guide you to understanding and addressing these issues, and ultimately, to develop a healthier self-view and realign our thoughts about food.

5.1 Unpacking the Impact of Body Image on Eating Habits

Body Image and Emotional Eating

Negative body image isn't just about dissatisfaction with one's appearance; it is deeply intertwined with emotional eating. When you feel uncomfortable in your skin, food can temporarily numb or soothe those painful feelings. It's like putting a Band-Aid on a wound without ever treating the infection. You might find yourself reaching for comfort foods after a negative comment about your weight or during times when you feel particularly insecure about your body.

This coping mechanism, while providing short-term relief, often leads to a cycle of guilt and further negative feelings about one's body, fueling ongoing emotional eating. Identifying and recognizing this pattern marks the initial step toward healing. It helps you understand that emotional eating driven by body dissatisfaction doesn't address the deeper issues of self-esteem and body acceptance.

Societal Influences

Our perceptions of our bodies do not exist in a vacuum. They are heavily influenced by societal standards and media representations that often glorify a narrow, usually unattainable standard of beauty. These influences can make us feel as though our bodies are problems to be fixed, with every magazine promising the next solution to lose weight or change our shape. For instance, have you ever felt pressured to look a certain way because of a celebrity's appearance on a magazine cover?

This constant barrage can lead to a preoccupation with body image, making food a tool for achieving these unrealistic ideals rather than a source of nourishment and enjoyment. It's crucial to critically analyze these societal influences and recognize their impact on our self-perception and eating behaviors. By challenging these external pressures and focusing on health and wellness rather than appearance, we can reclaim our body image and relationship with food.

Personal Reflection

Reflecting on your own body image can be an illuminating exercise. Take a moment to think about how you view your body and how this view affects your eating habits.

Do you eat certain foods or avoid others based on how you feel about your body?

Do you punish or reward yourself with food based on your appearance?

Understanding your own patterns is vital to breaking the cycle of emotional eating linked to body image. This reflection isn't about judging yourself but about gaining insight into how your perceptions have shaped your behaviors and how you might start to change these patterns.

QUIZ Here's another exercise that can help you assess your tendencies towards body image-related emotional eating.

For each of these questions, choose your answer: Rarely/Never? Sometimes? Often? Always?

1. How often do you compare your body to others, especially in a negative light?

2. Do you find yourself avoiding social situations or events because of how you feel about your body?

3. Have you ever engaged in extreme dieting or exercise to change your body shape due to dissatisfaction with your appearance?

4. Do you experience guilt, shame, or anxiety after eating certain foods because of how they make you feel about your body?

5. How frequently do you use food as a way to cope with negative emotions or stress related to your body image?

Scoring System:

For each question, assign the following points based on your answer:

- 0 points for "Rarely/Never"
- 1 point for "Sometimes"
- 2 points for "Often"
- 3 points for "Always"

Scoring Interpretation

- 0-4 points: Low likelihood of body image issues leading to emotional eating habits.
- 5-9 points: Moderate likelihood of body image issues leading to emotional eating habits.
- 10-14 points: High likelihood of body image issues leading to emotional eating habits.
- 15-20 points: Very high likelihood of body image issues leading to emotional eating habits.

Starting the Journey to Positive Body Image

The journey toward a positive body image begins with challenging the negative thoughts and beliefs you hold about your body. Begin by challenging the validity of these thoughts. Are they based on unrealistic standards? Are they helping you live a healthier, happier life? Often, the answer is no.

Cultivating gratitude for your body's capabilities can also redirect your attention from how your body looks to its functionalities. Whether it's appreciating your legs for carrying you through a morning run or your arms for holding your loved ones, acknowledging the functionality of your body can foster a greater appreciation and a more positive body image.

Gratitude Journaling Prompt

ACTION To deepen this practice, add a section in your gratitude journal, focused on your body. Each day, write down three things your body enables you to do. For example, "Today, I enjoyed my time walking the dog" , "I'm thankful for my body and energy to tidy up the messy closet" or simply "Today, I am thankful for my healthy body, and I will rest and enjoy a quiet Me-Time". This practice helps shift your focus from body appearance to body functionality, reducing the power of negative body image and its impact on your eating habits.

By understanding the profound link between how we perceive our bodies and how we eat, and reshaping this relationship through reflection and gratitude, we can pave the way for healthier, more joyful eating habits and a more compassionate self-view.

This transformation is not just about improving our eating habits; it's about enhancing our overall well-being and moving toward a life where food is a source of nourishment and pleasure, not a battleground for body image issues. Change is not only possible, but it's also within your reach, and your journey toward loving your body and appreciating food starts here.

5.2 Cultivating Body Positivity and Self-Acceptance

Embracing body positivity is like opening your arms wide to the diversity and beauty of all body types, including your own. It's about shifting from a critique-focused view to one of acceptance and celebration. This concept isn't merely a passing trend but an essential aspect of recovering from emotional eating.

When you feel good about your body, regardless of size or shape, you're less likely to seek comfort in food to cope with body dissatisfaction. Instead, you start to nourish it with kindness and respect, which can profoundly change your eating habits and overall health.

Cultivating body positivity and self-acceptance is a journey that leads to a positive and compassionate view of yourself. Don't forget that your body is unique, and it deserves your love, respect, and most importantly, your acceptance.

Body positivity roots itself in the understanding that all bodies are good bodies. It challenges the conventional beauty standards that often lead to a narrow, unachievable ideal. This acceptance helps mitigate the feelings of inadequacy that drive many of us to emotional eating. It allows for a more compassionate internal dialogue that celebrates your body's strength and resilience rather than critiquing it for not fitting a specific mold.

To cultivate this positive body image, incorporate daily *affirmations (more in chapter 5.4)* into your routine. These can be simple statements that reinforce body acceptance, such as "My body deserves respect and care" or "I am more than my appearance" or "I am grateful for my body and all it does for me". Say these affirmations out loud every morning, or write them in a journal. Over time, these positive affirmations can help reshape your perceptions, making it easier to see and appreciate the beauty in yourself just as you are.

Mindfulness also plays a significant role in fostering body positivity. It involves being present and fully experiencing the moment without judgment. Apply this to how you view your body. Instead of scanning for flaws, try observing your body with neutrality and kindness. When negative thoughts arise, acknowledge them without attachment and gently redirect your focus to qualities you appreciate about your body. This could be anything from the softness of your skin to the way your body supports you in daily activities.

Celebrating body diversity is another essential aspect of body positivity. It's about recognizing and appreciating various human forms, each with its own beauty and uniqueness. This celebration can be as simple as complimenting others on non-physical traits, supporting brands that showcase diverse body types, or participating in communities that affirm body positivity. By seeing and valuing diversity in others, you can also begin to appreciate it yourself.

Navigating the days when body positivity feels out of reach is also part of this process. We all have moments of doubt or criticism toward our bodies. During these times, focus on self-care and compassion. Engage in activities that make you feel good physically and emotionally, whether that's a soothing bath, a favorite hobby, or a walk in nature.

Remind yourself of your body's capabilities and the positive experiences it allows you to have. Having a support system, such friends, family, or online communities that uplift and affirm body positivity is also helpful. Lean on these supports when your own resolve wavers.

Cultivating a positive body image is a nurturing process that benefits your mental and physical health. It encourages a joyful and satisfying connection with food, one that is based on nourishment rather than punishment. This shift doesn't happen overnight, but each step you take toward accepting and celebrating your body contributes to a more balanced, contented life.

As you continue to practice body positivity, just bear in mind that everybody has a good body, and your body is no exception. Through acceptance and celebration, you can transform how you see yourself and how you live in and enjoy the world.

5.3 The Media and Body Image: Developing Critical Viewing Skills

In an age where media is as ubiquitous as the air we breathe, it's no surprise that its powerful currents shape our views, including how we perceive our bodies. The images we consume daily, from billboards to Instagram feeds, aren't just passive visuals; they actively influence our self-esteem and body image, often setting an unrealistic and uniform bar.

Developing critical viewing skills is like putting on a pair of glasses to help you see the media landscape more clearly, recognizing the distortion, and deciding for yourself what reflects your values and truth.

Media literacy *(mentioned in chapter 1.4)* is about learning to question and analyze the media content we consume rather than taking it at face value. It involves understanding the motives behind media productions — acknowledging that every magazine cover, every fashion ad, and every influencer post is crafted with specific goals, often aimed at selling something, be it a product or an idea. This understanding is crucial because once you recognize the intention, you can better guard against its influence.

Start by identifying the common themes in the images or messages. Do they suggest that beauty has a specific size, shape, or color? Are they implying that happiness or success comes from looking a certain way? By asking these questions, you can initiate the process of separating your self-esteem from these commercially-driven standards.

The role that social media plays in shaping body image is particularly potent. Platforms like Instagram and Facebook are fraught with curated realities; the feeds are filled with perfect moments, bodies, and seemingly perfect lives. This curation can lead to the comparison trap, where you measure your body and life against those idealized snapshots, often feeling inadequate or dissatisfied. It's important to remember that what you're seeing is a selected display of highlights, not the whole story.

Everyone has struggles and insecurities, no matter how flawless their feed appears. To counteract the negative impact of social media on body image, make a conscious effort to engage with it mindfully. Ask yourself how you feel after scrolling through certain feeds. If you notice that you feel worse about yourself, it might be time to clean up your digital environment.

Curating a positive media feed is about being selective with what you allow into your digital space.

- Follow accounts that promote body diversity and positivity.

- Look for content creators who share realistic images and messages that resonate with authenticity and inclusiveness.

- Diversifying your feed can reduce feelings of body inadequacy and expose you to a more enriching range of perspectives and ideas.

- Seek hashtags or groups that celebrate body positivity and connect with communities supporting your self-acceptance journey.

By populating your feed with positive influences, you emphasize the idea that beauty is diverse and your worth and value are not tied to your appearance or how you look.

As you continue to navigate your media-rich environment, don't forget that you have the power to choose what you consume and what you believe about yourself. These choices can empower you to maintain a positive body image, free from the confines of unrealistic standards and expectations, fostering a healthier, more joyful engagement with your digital and real-life worlds.

5.4 Body Image Healing Practices: From Affirmations to Self-Care Routines

Consider this: starting each day with a gentle whisper of kindness directed toward yourself, affirmations that build and reinforce a foundation of self-acceptance and love. These affirmations are not just words; they are powerful tools for healing your perception of your body and enhancing your relationship with yourself. Incorporating affirmations focused on body acceptance into your daily routine can significantly shift your internal dialogue from criticism to appreciation, profoundly impacting your self-esteem and eating habits.

Affirmations for body acceptance are simple, positive statements you repeat to yourself, designed to foster a positive relationship with your body. They serve as reminders of your worth, beauty, and strength, regardless of your shape or size. For instance, starting your day by looking in the mirror and affirming, "My body is beautiful and deserves respect," or "I am worthy of love and kindness, no matter my size," can set a positive tone for the day.

These affirmations help in rerouting old paths of negative self-talk and body shaming, creating new, positive trails in your mind. It's about changing the narrative from one of inadequacy to one of celebration and acceptance. Over time, this shift can ease the emotional distress that often leads to emotional eating as you start to feel more comfortable and confident in your body.

Self-care *(refer to chapter 7.5)* plays a significant role in cultivating a positive body image; it refers to those intentional actions that you take to care for physical, emotional, and spiritual well-being. In the context of body image, self-care practices can help you cultivate a more compassionate and appreciative relationship with your body. This might look like engaging in physical activities you enjoy, which celebrate rather than punish your body. Whether dancing, yoga, or a quiet walk in nature, these activities can help you connect with and appreciate your body's capabilities.

Emotional self-care might involve setting aside time for activities that soothe and recharge your spirit, such as spending time with people you love, reading a book, or meditating. Spiritually, it might mean engaging in practices connecting you to a larger purpose or your values through religious activities, meditation, or time in nature.

Customizing your self-care routine is key to making it practical and sustainable. It should be tailored to fit your unique needs, preferences, and lifestyle. Start by identifying what aspects of your life need more attention and what activities bring you the most joy and relaxation. If your mornings are rushed, waking up a bit earlier to have a quiet coffee might feel nurturing. If you find joy in creativity, scheduling regular time for sketching or writing could be your form of self-care.

The goal is to design a routine that supports all aspects of your well-being, making it easier to maintain a positive body image and healthy eating habits.

The connection between a consistent self-care routine and eating habits is profound. When you regularly follow this routine, you effectively reduce the stress and emotional turbulence that often lead to emotional eating. Self-care provides alternative ways to cope with emotions that don't involve food, offering you a variety of tools to manage stress, boredom, or loneliness.

For example, if you're feeling stressed, you might unwind with a yoga session or a creative activity instead of turning to snacks. This helps manage your immediate stress and builds resilience over time, minimizing the chances of turning to food for emotional comfort.

By integrating affirmations and a personalized self-care routine into your daily routine, you actively nurture a positive body image and create a positive attitude toward food. This approach supports not just your physical health but enriches your emotional and spiritual well-being, contributing to a more balanced and joyful life.

A Personal Note from the Author

"As you grow older, you will discover that you have two hands, one for helping yourself, the other for helping others."
~ Audrey Hepburn

Wow, you've made it this far, well done! Thank you so much for joining me on this journey through understanding and managing emotional eating; I'm honored to be a part of it.

If you've found the insights and strategies mentioned in this book helpful and empowering, if something has resonated with you or made a positive impact, I'd love to hear your thoughts by reviewing this book.

Imagine others out there, much like you were, before discovering this book. They are seeking guidance as they strive to overcome emotional eating, but they're unsure where to turn. With a simple act of kindness, you can make a real difference in their search for help, and you can do this by leaving your review of this book.

Reviews are more than just feedback; they are beacons for those searching in the dark. By sharing your thoughts you are guiding someone to a potential life-changing resource.

Your words have power. I would be incredibly grateful if you spare a few moments to share your experience in a review.

Simply scan this QR code to leave your review on Amazon or go to: https://amzn.to/4bgXcpW

Helping others always leaves us with that wonderful, warm and fuzzy 'feel-good' feeling, knowing we've contributed to someone's betterment. Let's spread that joy together.

Thank you from the bottom of my heart for your kind support. Okay, let's move on to the next chapter about building your own toolkit to build emotional resilience.

With heartfelt gratitude,

Kitty Barrett

Chapter 6
Building a Toolkit for Emotional Resilience

"Self-discipline begins with the mastery of your thoughts. If you don't control what you think, you can't control what you do."
~ Napoleon Hill

The path to conquering emotional eating can be challenging and trying. Therefore, you need to build your resilience to fight through this battle in order to build a healthy relationship with food and your body. This chapter is about building your own toolkit — an emotional resilience kit that helps you navigate those tough moments without turning to the pantry.

6.1 Your Emotions Without Food

Tools for identifying and naming emotions accurately.

It all starts with understanding what you're really feeling. Can you tell the difference between feeling bored and feeling lonely? How about distinguishing stress from anxiety? It might sound straightforward, but so many of us go through our days not truly understanding our emotional states, which can lead us to make choices that don't actually address our needs.

Labeling Emotions

STRATEGY Have you ever felt overwhelmed by a whirlwind of emotions swirling inside you? It's like finding your way in the dark without a torch light. Here's a little secret that can make a big difference: labeling your emotions.

Labeling emotions is like giving a name to the different colors of your emotional palette. It's about identifying and acknowledging what you're feeling, whether it's joy, sadness, anger, or something in between. By putting words to your emotions, you gain clarity and insight into your inner world.

This practice can help reduce emotional intensity, almost like airing out a room and getting rid of stuffiness.

- You can start by checking in with yourself at different times throughout the day.

- Ask yourself, "What am I feeling right now?" Try to be as specific as possible. Instead of just saying you're stressed, identify whether you're feeling overwhelmed, frustrated, or underappreciated.

But it's not just about naming feelings; it's about understanding them. When you label an emotion, you create distance from it, allowing you to observe it more objectively. This simple act of recognition can help you manage your emotions more effectively and make wiser choices in how you respond.

Step-By-Step Guide to Practicing Labeling Emotions

Pause and Acknowledge: Whenever you notice a strong emotion arising, take a moment to pause whatever you're doing. Acknowledge that you're experiencing an emotion and give yourself permission to explore it without judgment.

Tune into Sensations: Bring your awareness to your body and notice any physical sensations associated with the emotion. Is there tightness in your chest, a knot in your stomach, or a sense of lightness or heaviness somewhere? Tune into these sensations as they provide valuable clues about your emotional state.

Identify the Emotion: Now, try to label the emotion you're feeling. Is it joy, sadness, anger, fear, excitement, or something else? Use words that resonate with your inner experience. For example, instead of simply saying, "I feel bad," you might say, "I'm feeling anxious about the upcoming presentation."

Validate Your Emotion: Once you've identified the emotion, validate it. Remind yourself that it's okay to feel this way; emotions are a natural part of being human. Avoid judging yourself or trying to suppress the emotion. Validate your experience with kindness and self-compassion.

Explore the Root Cause: If you're comfortable, take a moment to explore the root cause of the emotion. Ask yourself why you might be feeling this way. Is there a specific trigger, past experience, or underlying belief contributing to the emotion? This deeper exploration can offer valuable insights into your emotional patterns.

Express Emotion Appropriately: Depending on the situation, consider how you can express the emotion in a healthy and constructive way. This might involve talking to a trusted friend, journaling about your feelings, engaging in creative expression, or simply allowing yourself to feel the emotion without resistance.

Practice Mindfulness: Throughout this process, practice mindfulness by staying present with your emotions without getting swept away by them. Notice any tendencies to over identify with the emotion or get caught up in stories about it. Stay grounded in the present moment and the physical sensations associated with the emotion.

Reflect on the Experience: After labeling and exploring your emotion, take a moment to reflect on the experience. Notice any shifts in your emotional state or insights gained from the practice. Consider what you learned about yourself and how to apply this awareness in future emotional situations.

Repeat as Needed: Emotions are dynamic and ever-changing, so feel free to repeat this labeling practice whenever you encounter strong emotions. The more you practice, the more familiar you'll become with your emotional landscape, enhancing your emotional and self-awareness.

Remember, labeling emotions is not meant to suppress or eliminate them but to develop a deeper understanding and relationship with your inner world. Embrace the process with curiosity, compassion, and openness to growth.

So, next time you're riding the rollercoaster of emotions, take a moment to pause, breathe, and label what you're feeling. It's a small yet powerful tool that empowers you to navigate life's ups and downs with greater awareness and resilience.

Separating Emotion from Action: Teach how to feel emotions without acting on them impulsively, particularly with eating.

Once you've identified your emotions, the next step is learning not to act on them impulsively. This is where real resilience is built. Let's say you identify that you're feeling anxious; the typical response might be to distract or soothe yourself with food because it's quick and available. But what if you paused and thought about what might really help reduce your anxiety? Maybe it's taking a walk, calling a friend, or writing down what's making you anxious.

This pause is crucial; it's about creating a space between your feelings and your actions. Think of it as emotional agility, being able to sit with your feelings without being driven by them. One way to practice this is by implementing a 'mindful check-in' before meals. Before you start eating, take a moment to assess your emotional state. Ask yourself, "Am I eating because I'm hungry, or is there something else going on?" Recognize and acknowledge your emotions if they drive your desire to eat, and consider what other actions might address those feelings more effectively.

Emotional Reflection Exercise

ACTION

This exercise isn't about denying yourself food, it's about making sure that eating is what you genuinely need at that moment.

- Next time you feel driven to eat emotionally, take a five-minute break before you give in.

- During these five minutes, write down what you're feeling and why.

- Then, brainstorm three other actions you could take that might address this emotion.

By getting better at identifying your emotions and separating them from your actions, you empower yourself to make choices that genuinely nourish you — not just in the moment but in ways that contribute to your long-term happiness and health. It's about building a relationship with yourself where you understand and respect your emotional landscape, navigating through it with awareness and grace.

This toolkit isn't just for managing eating habits: It's for enriching your life, making you more resilient and responsive to life's ups and downs. As you continue to practice these skills, you'll find that they become second nature, transforming not just how you eat but how you live.

6.2 Mindfulness Practices for Interrupting Emotional Eating Episodes

Mindfulness might sound like a buzzword often tossed around in wellness circles, but as we've learned earlier in chapters, it's actually a powerful tool that can radically change how you interact with food. It's all about bringing your full attention to the present moment, which is incredibly helpful when emotions threaten to take over your eating habits.

By increasing your awareness, you can catch those moments when emotional hunger tries to masquerade as physical hunger, allowing you to make more conscious choices about how you respond.

The fundamentals: mindfulness involves observing without judgment. It means not forming any opinions and just being present in the moment. It's about noticing your thoughts, feelings, and bodily sensations as they are, not as you think they should be. This can be particularly enlightening when it comes to eating. For instance, you might notice that the urge to snack pops up when you're not actually hungry but rather feeling lonely or bored. The first step in breaking the cycle of emotional eating is to recognize this pattern.

Breathing Exercises

A straightforward method to develop mindfulness is through focused breathing exercises. When it comes to managing your eating triggers, these can be a game-changer. Before you reach for that snack, try this:

- Take a deep breath in.
- Count to four.
- Hold it for a count of four.
- Exhale slowly for another four.

This type of breathing helps center your mind and body, making it easier to assess whether you're truly hungry or just reacting to your emotions. It acts like a pause button, giving you a moment to reflect on your feelings and why you might be feeling it. Over time, this practice can help you develop a more mindful approach to eating, where choices are made deliberately, not out of habit or impulse.

Mindful Pause

Now, let's talk about the 'mindful pause.' This is a deliberate break you take before you begin to eat, primarily when you feel driven by emotions rather than hunger. During this pause, sit with your feelings for a moment. Ask yourself, "What's really going on here? Am I hungry, or am I perhaps feeling something else that's prompting me to eat?"

This isn't about making you feel guilty for wanting to eat; it's about developing a deeper understanding of your eating habits. It's about giving yourself the chance to make a different choice, one that addresses your emotional needs more directly.

Grounding Techniques

Grounding techniques are another cornerstone of mindfulness that can be especially useful if you find your emotions overwhelming. These techniques are designed to help you stay present and reduce the intensity of emotional distress. A simple yet effective grounding method involves using your five senses. Look around and list:

- Five things you can see
- Four things you can hear
- Three things you can touch
- Two things you can smell

- One thing you can taste

This practice not only diverts your attention away from emotional eating triggers but also brings you back to the present moment, making it easier to make a mindful choice about food.

Incorporating these mindfulness practices into your daily schedule doesn't need to be complex or time-consuming. It can be as simple as taking a few deep breaths before each meal, pausing to check in with yourself, or using grounding techniques when you feel triggered. Consistency is crucial.

The more you engage in mindfulness exercises, the more innate they'll feel, leading to a more substantial impact on managing emotional eating. It's about building a toolkit that you can draw from whenever you feel that old, familiar urge to find comfort in food. With each mindful practice, you're not just avoiding unnecessary eating but also fostering a deeper, more compassionate understanding of yourself and your needs.

6.3 The Power of Movement & Exercise in Emotional Well-Being

Let's talk about the magic of movement and how it can be a game-changer for your emotional well-being. It not only helps to burn calories and build muscles, but it also helps to clear your mind and lift your spirits. Regular physical activity can be a fantastic stress reliever, acting almost like a pressure valve, releasing built-up tension that, if left unchecked, might lead you straight to emotional eating.

When you exercise, your body releases endorphins, those wonderful chemicals known as the body's natural painkillers and mood elevators. Imagine finishing a brisk walk or a dance class; you're not just working your body; you're also bathing your brain in these feel-good chemicals, often leading to what's known as the 'runner's high'. This natural boost can significantly counteract stress and reduce the likelihood of you reaching for comfort food as a stress response.

The link between exercise and mood improvement is well-supported by research. Engaging in regular physical activity leads to improving our moods and reducing symptoms of depression and anxiety. Think of it as a natural antidepressant.

When you're feeling down or anxious, instead of isolating or eating out of emotion, getting up and moving can shift your perspective and alleviate negative feelings. It's about channeling the energy that your emotions bring into physical activity, transforming it into a force for good in your body and mind. This doesn't mean you need to engage in intense workouts; even moderate, enjoyable activities like cycling, yoga, or gardening can uplift your mood and improve your emotional resilience.

TIPS Listening to your body's needs and limits in exercise is critical. We often fall into the trap of thinking more is always better, but this isn't the case with physical activity, especially when you're using it as a tool to manage emotional well-being. It's essential to tune into your body and recognize the signs it gives you.

- If you're feeling energized and strong, it's a good day for a more challenging workout.

- But if you're tired or sore, it might be a day for gentle stretching or a leisurely walk.

This act of listening and responding to your body prevents physical burnout and teaches you a form of respect and care for your body that can translate into how you manage emotions and stress.

Incorporating additional physical activity into your daily routine may seem daunting, especially when you're juggling a million other responsibilities. However, the emotional benefits are so compelling that finding ways to weave movement into your day is worth it.

- Start with small, manageable changes.

- If you spend much time at a desk, try standing or stretching every hour, or utilize part of your lunch break for a quick walk.

- Opt for the stairs instead of the elevator.

- Consider doing light exercises like yoga or Pilates while you enjoy your favorite TV shows in the evenings.

These small integrations can add up to significant emotional and physical benefits over time, enhancing your mood and reducing your stress levels.

The connection between the mind and body is robust and complex, and strengthening this connection through exercise can lead to profound improvements in how you relate to food and handle emotional challenges. Regular physical activity helps fortify this mind-body connection, making you more attuned to the signals your body sends about hunger, stress, and emotional needs. This heightened awareness can help you make better choices about eating, choosing to nourish rather than feed, and using food for sustenance rather than emotional comfort.

As you continue to build and rely on this toolkit of movement and exercise, you'll likely find a more balanced approach to managing your emotions, one that supports both your mental and physical health in a harmonious and sustainable way.

6.4 Cultivating Self-Compassion & Self-Care: A Journey to Self-Love

Understanding self-compassion might be the game-changer in how you approach not only your eating habits but also how you navigate the ups and downs of everyday life. Self-compassion is the art of treating yourself with the same kindness, concern, and support you would offer a good friend. It's recognizing that it's okay to be imperfect, to struggle, and to feel pain.

When it comes to eating and body image, self-compassion shifts your perspective from criticism to understanding, allowing you to navigate setbacks with a supportive mindset rather than a punitive one.

Suppose you had a day where everything seemed to go wrong, and you ended up eating way past your point of comfort. Without self-compassion, this might spiral into a night of berating yourself, a cascade of self-critical thoughts that not only deepen your distress but might also set you up for more emotional eating.

Now, let's flip that script with self-compassion. In this version, you acknowledge that you were having a tough day and that eating was a way you tried to cope. You offer yourself understanding and remind yourself that everyone has moments of struggle. This kind of response can ease your distress and open up a space where you can consider more supportive reactions in the future.

Self-care extends this concept into action. It's often narrowly depicted as treating yourself to a spa day or indulging in a fancy meal. While these can certainly be aspects of self-care, at its core, self-care is about regular practices that maintain and enhance your health and well-being, both mentally and emotionally. It means setting boundaries around work so you don't burn out, ensuring you get enough sleep, staying hydrated, connecting with loved ones, and allowing yourself to enjoy food without guilt.

Incorporating self-care activities that don't revolve around food is vital, especially if food has been your go-to way to relieve stress or manage emotions. Consider activities that nourish you not just physically but also emotionally and spiritually. This could be something as simple as scheduling a regular time each day to unwind with a book, taking up a new hobby like painting or gardening, or practicing yoga or meditation. These activities aren't just about distraction; they enrich your life and provide fulfillment and joy.

Daily Self-Care (Self-Love) Checklist

We all know that life can be hectic, and time is so precious especially when you're juggling work, kids, and everything in between. It's easy to put yourself on the back burner, but self-love is crucial — even more so when you're constantly on the go.

This Daily Self-Love Checklist is designed to help you squeeze in moments of self-care throughout your day without feeling overwhelmed. Each activity is quick, easy, and can be seamlessly integrated into your routine.

Whether you're getting ready in the morning, taking a quick break at work, or winding down before bed, these small acts of self-love can make a big difference in how you feel about yourself. Remember, it's not about finding extra time in your already packed schedule; it's about making the most of the little moments you have.

So, let's embark on this journey together to banish body negativity and start truly loving ourselves, one tiny step at a time. You deserve it!

Morning

- **Positive Affirmations:** Start your day by looking in the mirror and saying three positive affirmations about yourself.

- **Gratitude Journaling:** Write down three things you are grateful for in your body and life.

- **Gentle Stretching:** Spend 5-10 minutes doing gentle stretches to wake up your body and show appreciation for its capabilities.

- **Hydrate:** Drink a glass of water to nourish and hydrate your body first thing in the morning.

Mid-Morning

- **Mindful Breathing**: Take a 5-minute break to focus on your breath, grounding yourself and reducing any stress or anxiety.

- **Healthy Snack:** Choose a nutritious snack, such as fruit or nuts, to fuel your body and mind.

- **Compliment Yourself:** Write down one thing you love about your body or something it has done for you recently.

Lunchtime

- **Balanced Meal:** Prepare or choose a balanced meal that includes a variety of nutrients to nourish your body.

- **Mindful Eating:** Eat slowly, savoring each bite, and paying attention to the flavors and textures of your food.

- **Positive Media Consumption:** Listen to a podcast, read an article, or watch a video that promotes body positivity and self-love.

Afternoon

- **Physical Activity:** Engage in a physical activity you enjoy, whether it's a walk, yoga, dancing, or a workout, to celebrate your body's abilities.

- **Progress Acknowledgment:** Reflect on any progress you've made in your self-love journey, no matter how small, and celebrate your efforts.

- **Connection:** Reach out to a friend or loved one to share a positive thought or simply connect and uplift each other.

Evening

- **Relaxation Ritual:** Create a relaxation routine, such as taking a warm bath, meditating, or reading a favorite book, to unwind and show care for your mental well-being.

- **Reflective Journaling:** Write down three positive things that happened today and how they made you feel, focusing on your accomplishments and moments of joy.

- **Body Appreciation:** Before bed, thank your body for everything it has done for you today. Focus on the functions and capabilities rather than appearance.

- **Set Intentions:** Set a positive intention for the next day, something you aim to achieve or a way you want to feel, to cultivate ongoing self-love and positivity.

Tips for Using the Checklist:

- Customize the checklist to fit your lifestyle and preferences.

- Consistency is key — try to incorporate these activities into your daily routine.

- Be kind and patient with yourself; self-love is a journey, not a destination.

- Celebrate your progress and recognize your efforts regularly.

Practices for Developing Self-Compassion

ACTION: Developing a more *compassionate dialogue* with yourself is a practice that takes time and intention. Start by noticing when you're being self-critical, especially around eating or body image.

- What are the things you're saying to yourself?

- Would you ever say the same thing to someone else you care about? Probably not.

- Try to gently challenge these thoughts. Replace them with kinder, more supportive messages. For instance, if you find yourself thinking, "I shouldn't have eaten that; I'm so weak," you might replace it with, "It's okay that I ate that. It's human to seek comfort, and I'm learning to cope in different ways."

Another powerful practice is *writing a letter to yourself* from the perspective of a compassionate friend. This helps you realize the harshness of your self-judgments and discover a kinder, more understanding way to relate to yourself.

- Write about your struggles with food and body image, then

- Respond with empathy, encouragement, and understanding.

This can help you internalize a more compassionate perspective and apply it in daily life.

Self-Compassion and Body Image

Cultivating self-compassion can lead to significant shifts in how you view your body. It encourages you to appreciate your body for what it can do rather than criticizing it for how it looks. This shift from a critical to a caring perspective can reduce the body dissatisfaction that often triggers emotional eating. It allows for a more accepting and respectful relationship with your body, one that honors its needs and appreciates its strengths.

For instance, instead of fixating on losing weight or achieving a certain look, self-compassion guides you to focus on behaviors that enhance your health and well-being. This might mean choosing to eat nutritious foods because they make you feel good, not because they'll help you fit into a smaller size. It's about exercising to celebrate your body's capabilities, not to punish it for its imperfections.

In this way, self-compassion and self-care are not just strategies for better eating habits but approaches to living more fully and kindly. They enable you to navigate life's challenges including those related to food and body image — with greater ease and support. As you cultivate these practices, you may find that they transform your relationship with food, enhancing your quality of life, which leads to greater contentment and a more profound sense of well-being.

6.5 Strategies for Managing Emotional Eating Without Dieting

When it comes to emotional eating, dieting often feels like the go-to solution. "Cut out the carbs", "Watch the sugars", and "Count every calorie". Sounds familiar, right? But here's the twist: for those of us who eat in response to stress or emotions, strict dieting can actually fuel the fire rather than extinguish it. It's like covering a cracked dam with a thin cement patch; it might seem to work temporarily, but eventually, the pressure will cause it to burst.

Quite often, dieting ignores the underlying emotional needs that lead to overeating, setting up a cycle of restriction, craving, and ultimately, binge eating. Instead of this restrictive approach, let's explore more compassionate, sustainable ways to address emotional eating.

The concept of intuitive eating *(as mentioned in chapter 4.2)* provides a refreshing alternative. This method encourages you to tune into your body's hunger and fullness cues instead of adhering to external diet rules. It's about relearning to trust your body's signal, something we might have lost along the way, especially if dieting has been part of our life for a long time.

Intuitive eating focuses on understanding your body's needs and responding to those needs without judgment. It involves recognizing the difference between physical hunger that needs nourishing and emotional hunger that might be better addressed with a walk, a good chat with a friend, or some quiet time. By tuning into your body's natural cues, you can start to eat in a way that satisfies you physically and emotionally without the guilt that often accompanies dietary restrictions.

Creating a flexible and forgiving approach to eating is necessary in this process. This means allowing all foods into your life but being mindful of what makes you feel good. It's about enjoying a slice of birthday cake at a party because it brings you joy, not just because it's there. It's about choosing a salad for lunch because it's crisp and refreshing, not because you 'should'. When food is no longer categorized strictly as 'good' or 'bad', it loses much of its emotional charge, making it easier to make choices based on nourishment and pleasure rather than compulsion or restriction.

An essential part of managing emotional eating is the environment you create around yourself — both physically and socially. A supportive environment can significantly impact your eating habits and your overall well-being. Physically, this might mean keeping your kitchen stocked with foods that nourish you and make you feel good. It's also about organizing your eating space to make it inviting and relaxing, encouraging mindful eating rather than distracting.

Socially, it involves surrounding yourself with people who understand and support your goals. This could mean sharing your approach with family and friends or connecting with a community or group who are on a similar path. Support can also come from professionals, like dietitians or therapists, who understand the challenges of emotional eating and can offer guidance and strategies tailored to your needs.

Embracing these strategies involves a shift from a diet-focused mindset to a more holistic, self-compassionate approach to eating and living. It's a move toward listening to and respecting your body, responding to its needs, and enjoying food as one of life's pleasures without anxiety or guilt. This approach helps manage emotional eating and positively shifts your mindset toward food, making eating a joyful, nourishing experience rather than a source of stress. As we wrap up this chapter, let's reflect on the key points we've covered.

We've explored the limitations of dieting when it comes to emotional eating, learned about self-compassion, and honored our body's natural cues. We've discussed the importance of creating a flexible, guilt-free approach to eating, and strategies are not just about changing how you eat; they're about building a healthy connection with food, from one of struggle to one of enjoyment and respect.

Chapter 7
Overcoming Setbacks and Maintaining Progress

"The best project you'll ever work on is you."

~ Sonny Franco

Picture this scenario: you've been diligently following your new eating and mindfulness plan. You're feeling great, healthier, and proud of your progress. Then, life throws a curveball — a stressful week at work or unexpected family issues. Suddenly, you find yourself seeking comfort in a pint of ice cream. The old habits resurface, and guilt washes over you. Sound familiar?

Let's be clear: Setbacks are a natural part of any change process, including your journey to conquer emotional eating. The key isn't to avoid these setbacks but to learn from them and bounce back more resiliently.

7.1 Identifying and Learning from Emotional Eating Setbacks

Recognizing Setbacks as Part of the Journey

First things first, let's normalize setbacks. Everyone experiences them, especially when making significant lifestyle changes. Think of setbacks not as failures but as inevitable steps to understanding and mastering your eating habits. They are not roadblocks but signposts that offer crucial insights into what triggers your emotional eating and why.

By shifting your perspective this way, you can lessen the guilt associated with setbacks and start to see them as opportunities for deeper learning and growth.

Analyzing the Setback

When you encounter a setback, it's essential to approach it with curiosity rather than judgment. Take a step back and analyze the situation.

- What triggered the emotional eating?
- Was it a specific event, a feeling, or perhaps a particular time of day?

Understanding the context of your setback is crucial. It's like being a detective in your own life, examining the clues to understand the 'why' behind your actions. This analysis is not about beating yourself up but about gathering the information you need to fortify your strategies against future challenges. Remember, setbacks are not just obstacles but valuable learning opportunities to help you go through this journey.

Adjusting Strategies

Armed with insights from your analysis, the next step is to adjust your coping strategies. Maybe you've realized that stress from work leads to late-night snacking. As a response, you may practice a relaxation method such as yoga or deep breathing exercises in the evening to address your stress before it drives you to the kitchen. Or perhaps you've noticed that boredom is a trigger, so you might plan engaging activities when you're likely to feel unoccupied.

The key here is flexibility. Your strategies should evolve as you learn more about your eating habits and triggers. This adaptive approach not only makes your plan more effective but also helps build resilience over time.

Recovery Strategies To Handle Setbacks

Some of these strategies may have already been mentioned in *chapter 3.6*, however, these are applicable specifically in helping you make adjustments to your own toolkit, to manage and recover from setbacks.

Practice Self-Compassion:

Possible Triggers: Self-Criticism, Perfectionism, Low Self-Esteem

Be kind to yourself and recognize that setbacks are a normal part of any recovery journey. Avoid self-criticism and negative self-talk. Instead, remind yourself that it's okay to have slip-ups and that each day is a new opportunity to make healthier choices.

Develop Healthy Coping Mechanisms:

Possible Triggers: Emotional Distress, Anxiety, Anger, Frustration

Replace emotional eating with healthier coping strategies. This might include activities such as going for a walk, practicing yoga, engaging in a hobby, or talking to a friend. Finding alternative ways to cope with emotions can reduce the likelihood of turning to food for comfort.

Mindful Eating Practices:

Possible Triggers: Distraction, Overeating, Lack of Awareness

Focus on eating mindfully by paying full attention to the eating experience. This includes eating slowly, savoring each bite, and listening to your body's hunger and fullness cues. Mindful eating can help you enjoy your food more and prevent overeating.

Seek Professional Support:

Possible Triggers: Underlying Emotional Issues, Chronic Stress, Trauma

Consider speaking with a therapist or a registered dietitian who specializes in emotional eating *(refer to chapters 6.3 and 7.4)*. Professional support can provide personalized strategies and accountability. Therapists can help address underlying emotional issues, while dietitians can offer practical advice on maintaining a balanced diet.

Engage in Stress-Relief Activities:

Possible Trigger: Stress

Identify when stress is triggering your emotional eating. Engage in activities that help reduce stress, such as meditation, deep breathing exercises, or taking a warm bath. Regularly incorporating stress-relief techniques into your routine can help manage stress levels and reduce the urge to eat emotionally.

Improve Sleep Hygiene:

Possible Trigger: Fatigue

Poor sleep can increase cravings for unhealthy foods and lower your ability to resist emotional eating. Improve your sleep hygiene by establishing a consistent sleep schedule, creating a relaxing bedtime routine, and ensuring your sleep environment is comfortable. Adequate rest can enhance your overall well-being and reduce emotional eating episodes.

Set Realistic Goals:

Possible Trigger: Frustration

Feeling frustrated with unrealistic goals can lead to emotional eating. Set achievable and realistic goals for yourself, whether they are related to eating habits, weight management, or personal achievements. Celebrate small victories along the way to keep motivation high and frustration at bay.

Create a Balanced Routine:

Possible Trigger: Boredom

Boredom can trigger emotional eating as a way to pass the time. Create a balanced daily routine that includes a variety of activities to keep you engaged and occupied. Incorporate hobbies, exercise, social activities, and productive tasks into your day. Having a structured and fulfilling routine can reduce the temptation to eat out of boredom.

Practice Gratitude:

Possible Trigger: Negativity or Low Mood

When feeling down or negative, it's easy to turn to food for comfort. Practicing gratitude can shift your focus to positive aspects of your life. Keep a gratitude journal and write down three things you're grateful for each day. This practice can improve your mood and reduce the tendency to eat in response to negative emotions.

Celebrating Recovery Efforts:

Lastly, always take a moment to celebrate your efforts to recover from a setback. Whether it's acknowledging your willingness to analyze what went wrong, making necessary adjustments, or simply not being too hard on yourself, every step deserves recognition. Celebrating these efforts reinforces your progress and bolsters your motivation to continue.

It's about acknowledging the strength it takes to get back up and keep moving forward, even in the face of challenges. This positive reinforcement is crucial in maintaining your progress and developing a healthy approach to eating.

Reflection Section

Now, let's put this into practice. Take a moment to reflect on a recent setback you experienced. Write down the specific details of what happened, how it made you feel, what you think triggered it, and one thing you might do differently next time. This practice of reflection can sharpen your awareness and enhance your ability to handle future setbacks more effectively.

Setbacks are not the end of the road; they are integral to the journey to a healthier, happier you. By learning to identify, analyze, adjust, and celebrate your recovery efforts, you equip yourself with the tools to navigate this path with confidence and resilience. Each step, each setback, and each recovery brings you closer to mastering your relationship with food and, most importantly, with yourself.

7.2 The Role of Self-Compassion in Overcoming Guilt and Shame

Understanding self-compassion isn't just about being nice to yourself; it's a profound tool that can reshape the way you handle setbacks, particularly those involving emotional eating. When setbacks happen, and you find yourself slipping back into old habits, the typical response might be to drown in guilt or wade through layers of shame. These feelings can be suffocating; without the right tools, they may lead you deeper into the cycles you're trying to escape.

Self-compassion offers a way out. It teaches you to treat yourself with the same understanding and kindness you would offer a good friend in a similar situation.

The concept of self-compassion involves three main components:

- Self-kindness: Refers to being warm and understanding toward ourselves rather than harshly critical.

- Common humanity: Involves understanding that suffering and personal failure are part of the shared human experience — they happen to everyone. In the context of emotional eating, this means that setbacks are not a personal failure but a common experience on the journey to a healthier food mindset.

- Mindfulness: In this context, mindfulness is about being present with your feelings of discomfort or failure without over-identifying with them.

When you embrace these aspects, the weight of guilt and shame begins to lift, not because your actions lack consequences but because you're learning to address them without destructive self-criticism.

One of the most effective ways to cultivate self-compassion is through specific exercises designed to enhance your understanding and practice of this critical skill. A powerful exercise for *self-compassion letter writing (mentioned in chapter 7.5)*.

Start by writing down what you feel guilty or ashamed about; be specific about the incident and your feelings.

- Then, write a letter to yourself from the perspective of a compassionate friend.

- This friend understands your struggles and sees your worth and goodness despite your mistakes.

- They offer comfort, perspective, and encouragement to find a way forward.

This exercise can be profoundly liberating because it allows you to step outside your self-critical thoughts and see yourself in a more balanced and compassionate light.

Another helpful practice is *self-kindness meditation.*

- Find a quiet space and a comfortable position.

- Start by focusing on your breath, then slowly direct your attention to the area around your heart.

- Imagine warmth and comfort emanating from this area, spreading through your body.

- As you bask in this warmth, speak kindly to yourself.

- Use phrases like 'May I be kind to myself' or 'May I accept myself as I am.'

This meditation can be particularly soothing during moments of intense self-criticism or after a setback. It's a reminder that you deserve kindness, especially from yourself, no matter what. This practice can help you cultivate self-compassion and develop a healthier relationship with yourself, which is essential in overcoming emotional eating.

Distinguishing between guilt and shame is crucial in applying self-compassion effectively. Guilt is feeling bad about something you've done, while shame is feeling bad about who you are. Guilt can be a constructive emotion, leading to positive change or making amends where needed.

Shame, however, is often destructive, attacking your self-worth and leading to feelings of inadequacy. Self-compassion mitigates both by shifting the focus from what you perceive as failings to understanding and accepting your human imperfections.

The power of forgiveness, particularly self-forgiveness (*refer to 'Letting Go' in chapter 2.2*), is a vital aspect of self-compassion. It involves letting go of self-directed anger and resentment toward oneself for past mistakes. Forgiveness doesn't mean you ignore or excuse your actions; instead, it means acknowledging them and forgiving yourself to move forward.

This can be incredibly freeing, especially if guilt and shame have kept you in a cycle of emotional eating. By forgiving yourself, you open up a space for growth and change, where setbacks are seen as part of the learning process, not proof of failure.

Embracing self-compassion may feel radical if you're used to self-criticism and guilt. However, its transformative potential is immense, not just in overcoming emotional eating but in all areas of life where you might harshly judge yourself. As you continue to practice self-compassion, you'll likely find that it not only changes how you relate to food but also how you relate to yourself and the world around you.

It's about building a kinder, more understanding relationship with yourself, where setbacks are met with kindness rather than criticism, and progress is celebrated in all forms, large and small.

7.3 Keeping a Progress Journal: Celebrating Successes, Big and Small

Let's talk about one of the most underrated yet powerful tools in your emotional eating toolkit: the progress journal. This can be a new journal, or you can also use the same food and mood diary or journal *(refer to chapter 2.6)*.

Reflect on this: being in your own personal space where you can unload your thoughts, celebrate your wins, and navigate your challenges more clearly. A progress journal serves just that purpose — it's a repository for your thoughts and feelings and a mirror reflecting your journey, helping you see patterns, progress, and areas needing attention.

Journaling as a Tool for Reflection

We have touched on journaling *(refer to chapter 2.6)*; journaling can be incredibly therapeutic. It's a way to process what you're going through, make sense of your emotions, and track your eating habits over time. But its benefits extend beyond mere documentation.

Through consistent journaling, you can see how far you've come, which is incredibly motivating on days when progress feels slow or invisible. It also lets you detect what triggers your emotional eating and identify what strategies are helping you cope better. Each entry enables you to tune in to your emotional state, offering insights into what affects your mood and food choices.

This self-reflection fosters a deeper understanding of your emotional needs and eating behaviors, making your efforts to overcome emotional eating more targeted and effective.

What to Include in Your Journal

The sky's the limit when it comes to what you can jot down in your progress journal, but here are a few pointers to get you started.

- First, consider tracking your emotional victories. These could be days when you chose a healthy coping mechanism over emotional eating or moments when you successfully identified and managed a trigger.

- Also, note changes in your habits. You may have started a new exercise routine, altered your diet to include more nutritious foods, or developed a bedtime ritual that helps you sleep better.

- Don't forget to document improvements in your physical health, too. Perhaps you feel more energetic, you're sleeping better, or your medical condition is improving. All these aspects provide a holistic view of your progress and are worth celebrating.

- Another valuable element to include is your emotional state. How did you feel today? Were there any highs or lows that influenced your eating habits?

- Additionally, reflecting on how certain foods make you feel physically and emotionally can guide you in making more mindful food choices in the future.

Try writing down your emotions to help you identify patterns and triggers, as this can help you develop strategies to manage them.

Celebrating Milestones

Setting and celebrating milestones is crucial in maintaining motivation. These milestones can be anything from sticking to a new eating plan for a whole week, managing a stressful day without turning to comfort food, or reaching a month of regular journaling.

Celebrating these achievements, big or small, reinforces positive behavior and keeps you engaged in your journey toward overcoming emotional eating.

Use your journal to reflect on these milestones.

- Write about how you achieved them
- How they made you feel, and
- What you learned from the experience.

This reflection not only boosts your morale but also deepens your commitment to your goals. It's a way of patting yourself on the back, recognizing your efforts and the strength it took to reach each milestone. Also, looking back at these entries can be incredibly uplifting and motivating on more challenging days, reminding you of what you can achieve.

Milestone Celebration Ideas

To make your milestone celebrations more tangible, here are a few ideas: For every major milestone, treat yourself to something special that doesn't involve food — maybe a new book, a small gift to yourself, a day out in nature, or a new experience like a pottery class. You could also create a 'victory jar' where you drop a note every time you hit a small milestone. Every month, read through these notes to remind yourself of all the progress you've made. These acts of celebration make your journey more enjoyable and embed a sense of achievement and positivity in your process.

Remember that the key to using a progress journal effectively is consistency. Make it a part of your daily routine; soon, it will become as natural as brushing your teeth. This journal is your personal space to explore, reflect, and celebrate. Embrace it fully and watch as it transforms your eating habits and relationship with yourself.

30-Day Emotional Eating Tracker

We all have those moments when we reach for a snack, not because we're hungry, but because we're feeling a bit emotional. Whether it's stress, boredom, or even happiness, our emotions can sometimes drive our eating habits in ways we don't even realize. That's why I've created this 30-Day Emotional Eating Tracking Chart for you.

This handy chart can help you uncover the mysteries behind your eating behaviors. By tracking your emotions, triggers, and eating patterns, you'll gain valuable insights into what drives you to eat when you're not really hungry. Think of it as a personal detective tool for your emotional eating habits. Let's dive in.

Scan this QR code or use the link below to download a digital copy of this chart: bit.ly/ee30DayTracker1

How to Use Your 30-Day Emotional Eating Tracking Chart

Daily Tracking:

Each day, take a few moments to jot down:

- **Triggers** (Emotion/Situation): Identify any events or situations that prompted you to reach for food. Was it an argument, a stressful meeting, or maybe just a dull afternoon? Or perhaps a specific emotion or situation that triggered the eating activity (e.g., stress, boredom, social gathering).

- **Eating Activity**: Description of the eating activity (e.g., snack, meal, binge).

- **Food Consumed**: Record what you ate when you felt these emotions. Was it a sugary treat, a salty snack, or something else?

- **Quantity/Serving Size:** Note the amount or serving size of the food consumed.

- **Emotions/Thoughts During Eating**: What were your thoughts or feelings while eating? Did you feel any guilt? Pleasure or distracted?

Weekly Reflection:

At the end of each week, take some time to reflect on your entries:

- **Patterns**: Look for any recurring themes or patterns in your eating habits.

- **Insights**: Consider what emotions or situations most likely trigger emotional eating.

- **Goals**: Set small, achievable goals for the next week to help manage your emotional eating. These could include finding alternative activities to distract yourself, practicing mindfulness, or reaching out for support.

30-Day Emotional Eating Tracking Chart

DAY #	DATE	TIME	TRIGGER	EATING ACTIVITY	FOOD CONSUMED	QUANTITY / SERVING	EMOTIONS / THOUGHTS
1							
2							
3							
4							
5							
6							
7							
8							
9							
10							
11							
12							
13							
14							
15							

7.4 Setting Boundaries Around Food

Navigating social eating scenarios, especially when trying to maintain healthy eating habits, can feel like walking a tightrope. You certainly don't want to end up in the land of stress-eating or post-party guilt. But what if you could attend these gatherings armed with strategies that help you enjoy the festivities while staying true to your eating goals? It starts with clear communication and a bit of pre-event strategizing.

Effective Communication Strategies

TIPS Communicating your dietary needs doesn't have to be a confrontation or an awkward whisper to the host. It's about being open and assertive with your needs while respecting the dynamics of the occasion. Begin by informing the host of your dietary preferences ahead of time.

This can be as simple as saying, "I'm excited to attend! I've been following a specific eating plan for health reasons, and I'd love to discuss how I can fit this into the meal planning. Maybe I can bring a dish that everyone can enjoy?" This approach not only eases your stress but also involves the host respectfully, making it a collaborative effort rather than a demand.

When it comes to expressing your needs at the event, keep it straightforward and positive. If offered something you prefer to avoid, a simple, "Thank you, but I'm actually full" or "I'm saving room for some of that delicious-looking salad!" provides a polite but firm boundary. Remember, you don't owe anyone a detailed explanation of your eating choices — being confident and polite is your best strategy.

Mindful Eating Techniques

Buffets, potlucks, and holiday meals are often a feast for the senses, making mindful eating challenging. Before you dive into the array:

1. Take a moment to pause and breathe.

2. Approach the buffet with the intention of selecting foods that genuinely appeal to you rather than trying a bit of everything out of a sense of obligation or impulse.

3. Fill your plate with small portions. This allows you to enjoy the taste of various items without overcommitting your appetite.

4. Try to focus on your food's taste, flavors, and textures as you eat, appreciating each bite.

Consuming your food slowly and savoring every mouthful enhances the experience and helps you tune into your body's fullness signals, preventing overeating.

After-Event Reflection

After attending special events or gatherings where food was served, take some time to reflect on your experience. Think about what went well and what could be improved next time. Did communicating your needs help you feel more in control of your eating? Were there moments when you felt pressured to eat out of politeness?

Reflecting on these questions can help you refine your strategies for future gatherings. This reflection is also an excellent opportunity to acknowledge your successes, no matter how small. Did you try a mindful eating technique? Did you communicate your needs effectively? Celebrating these victories can reinforce your confidence and commitment to healthy eating in social settings.

Journaling Prompt

This exercise will give you invaluable insights into your eating behaviors, which will help you develop effective eating strategies over time.

1. Start journaling about your experiences at social eating events.

2. Write about the emotions you felt, the challenges you faced, and how you handled them.

3. Describe what strategies worked and what didn't and how you might approach things differently in the future.

Navigating social eating doesn't have to feel like navigating a minefield. With clear communication, mindful eating techniques, and reflective practices, you can enjoy these gatherings fully without compromising your health goals or personal comfort.

7.5 Creating a Supportive Eating Environment

Creating a supportive eating environment starts right in the heart of your home: the kitchen. It's where decisions about what you eat, how much you eat, and even how you feel about eating are influenced daily.

Think of your kitchen as the command center for your eating habits. *Organizing* it in a way that promotes healthy eating can make a real difference in your daily life.

- Start by clearing your countertops of any high-calorie, low-nutrient snacks. Instead, place bowls of fresh fruit or pre-cut veggies with hummus on the counter. This simple switch can change what you reach for when looking for a quick bite.

- Next, take a look at your pantry and refrigerator. Rearrange them so that healthier options are front and center, and place less healthy items on higher or lower shelves, making them less immediately accessible.

This doesn't mean you can't have treats or indulgent foods at home, but you'll be more likely to think twice before grabbing them, ensuring they're a conscious choice rather than a convenience.

Cooking together is another wonderful way to foster a supportive atmosphere around food. It turns meal preparation from a chore into an enjoyable activity, and it's a perfect way to teach and learn healthy recipes.

- Whether it's with a partner, kids, or friends, involve them in the process.

- Let everyone choose a dish they'd like to try or assign tasks based on what each person enjoys; maybe someone loves chopping vegetables while another prefers measuring ingredients.

- This makes cooking more fun and educates everyone involved about the components of a healthy meal.

When you cook together, you're more likely to eat together, and this shared mealtime can strengthen relationships, encourage conversation, and slow down the pace of eating, allowing everyone to enjoy the food and feel more satisfied.

Seeking support from those around you who understand and respect your food choices is crucial. It's helpful to have open conversations with your family or housemates about why you're choosing to eat a certain way. Explain the reasons behind your decisions: perhaps for health reasons, to manage stress, or to feel better daily.

Helping others understand your motives, they're more likely to support you. This might mean agreeing not to bring certain trigger foods into the house or trying new healthy recipes together. Also, remind yourself that asking for support isn't a sign of weakness; it's a practical step toward creating a sustainable, healthy eating environment.

However, it's realistic to expect that not everyone will always be supportive. You might face backlash or misunderstandings from loved ones with different views about eating and health. It's essential to approach these situations patiently and keep communication open. Remain firm and focused in your commitment to your health, and listen to their concerns.

Often, backlash comes from a place of misunderstanding or fear that changes might affect your relationship. Reassure them that your choice to eat differently is not a judgment of their eating styles or an attempt to distance yourself from family traditions. Finding common ground where everyone feels heard and respected can help ease tensions and build mutual respect.

When creating a supportive home environment, remember that it's about more than just food — it's about setting up a space that minimizes stress and emotional triggers around eating. This might mean creating a pleasant dining area where you can eat without distractions or establishing a home routine that doesn't revolve around food but includes it in balanced ways. Maybe establish a family game night focusing on fun rather than food or organize regular outdoor activities that everyone enjoys.

As we wrap up this chapter, let's bear in mind that creating a supportive eating environment is about making thoughtful adjustments to your space and social interactions that encourage healthy eating habits. It involves organizing your kitchen to make healthy choices easier, cooking together to build skills and enjoy meals, seeking support from those around you, and handling any resistance with patience and understanding.

These steps aren't just about improving your diet; they're about enhancing the quality of your life at home, making it a place where healthy eating naturally aligns with how you live and interact with others. Keep these strategies in mind — they are foundational elements that can help you remain committed to a healthy lifestyle in a joyful and sustainable way.

7.6 Adjusting Your Strategy As Life Changes

Life, as you know, doesn't stand still. It ebbs and flows, bringing changes that sometimes sweep you off your feet. Whether it's a new baby, a job change, a move to a new city, or even the shifts that come with aging — each of these transitions can stir up emotions and disrupt your established routines, including how you manage emotional eating. Adapting your coping strategies to align with these life changes is helpful and necessary for maintaining your progress and emotional well-being.

Think about the last significant change you experienced. Perhaps it disrupted your meal planning routine or squeezed your 'me-time' into a thin sliver of hurried space. It's during such times that emotional eating can sneak back into your life, presenting itself as a quick comfort fix. Here's where the need for adaptability comes into play.

Begin by revisiting and adjusting your coping strategies to fit your new circumstances. Maybe your gym sessions need to shift to the morning because of work, or your meal prep days might need to change. It's about finding what works in your new normal.

Flexibility extends to your self-care routines as well. These routines need to be fluid, bending to accommodate the demands of your changing life. If you find your evenings are now too chaotic for a relaxing bath, a morning meditation can offer a similar relief. Or, if finding a full hour for a workout seems impossible, break it down into manageable 15-minute sessions throughout the day.

Self-care isn't a luxury; it's a crucial element that supports your emotional and physical health, helping you manage stress and reduce reliance on emotional eating.

Getting Professional Help

At times, despite your best efforts, you might find these transitions overwhelming, and that's perfectly okay. This might be the moment to consider seeking professional help. As mentioned in *chapter 6.3*, therapists, counselors, or dietitians can provide personalized strategies that address deeper underlying issues that might contribute to emotional eating. They can offer support and specific guidance tailored to your needs and circumstances, helping you navigate through your transitions more effectively.

Finding the right professional is like choosing a new friend; you need a good fit.

- Ask for referrals from people you know or trusted sources, or seek professionals specializing in emotional eating or life transitions.

- When you meet them, ask about their experience, their approach to treatment, and how they have helped others in similar situations.

- It's important that you feel comfortable and understood, as this relationship will be central to your progress.

Lastly, integrating professional advice into your life should feel enriching rather than overwhelming. Work with your chosen professional to identify practical steps that can be seamlessly incorporated into your current strategies. This might involve setting new goals, tweaking your meal plans, or introducing new coping mechanisms for stress. It's about enhancing your journey, providing you with tools and insights that fortify your resilience against emotional eating, no matter what life throws your way.

Navigating through life's changes can be challenging. Still, with the right strategies, flexibility, and professional guidance, you can maintain your progress and continue to develop a positive food mindset. Adapting isn't about losing your way in the face of change but evolving your strategies to meet life head-on, equipped with the tools and support you need to thrive through life's transitions.

7.7 Building a Long-Term Support Network & Community

When navigating the ups and downs of managing emotional eating, having a robust support network can be your anchor. It's comforting to know that there are others who share your experiences, and having people who understand and support your goals can make all the difference.

The journey toward overcoming emotional eating is filled with challenges. While personal resilience is crucial, the support of others can provide the strength and encouragement you need to stay the course, especially during tough times.

Building and maintaining a support network and community is essential for sustained success. Your network could include friends who listen without judgment, family members who encourage healthy habits, or professionals like therapists or dietitians who offer expert guidance. Each of these relationships contributes to a supportive environment that can help keep you motivated and accountable.

But how do you identify the right people to include in your support network?

- Start by evaluating your current relationships.
- Consider who makes you feel positive, supported, and understood.
- These are the people you want in your corner.
- It might be a friend who also struggles with emotional eating and understands your challenges or a family member who always

encourages you to take care of yourself.

When it comes to finding a community of like-minded individuals, it isn't just about having people to share recipes or workout tips with; it's about creating a network that resonates with your values, understands your struggles, and bolsters your commitment to a healthier you. The uniqueness of such a community is its diversity; people from various backgrounds sharing a common goal can offer different perspectives and solutions that perhaps you hadn't considered.

Support and connection doesn't only come from face-to-face interactions. Online forums, support groups, and community resources can be invaluable. These platforms allow you to connect with people from all over the world who are facing similar struggles. Engaging in online communities can provide insights and strategies that you might not have considered, and knowing what others go through, their struggles, and successes can be incredibly inspiring.

When choosing an online group, look for one focused on positivity, encouragement, and constructive advice. It's crucial that the space feels safe and welcoming so that you can share openly and benefit fully from the support offered.

The power of shared experiences in these communities cannot be overstated. There's immense strength derived from knowing you're not alone in your challenges. Group activities like cooking classes, group workouts, or even online workshops on nutrition and well-being can be incredibly empowering.

These shared experiences provide practical learning and emotional support, making the journey toward health less about individual struggle and more about collective triumph. They transform the path to health from a solitary trek to a group expedition where every member supports and uplifts others. It's about growing together and learning from each other's successes and setbacks.

Sustaining these relationships is just as important as forming them. Regular check-ins, whether they're casual coffee dates with a friend or scheduled appointments with a therapist, help keep your support network strong. These interactions provide an opportunity to discuss your progress, setbacks, and anything else affecting your emotional eating journey.

Mutual support is vital; just as you benefit from the encouragement of others, offering support and encouragement in return can strengthen your relationships and deepen your commitment to your goals. Establishing shared goals with your support network, like attending a healthy cooking class together or setting up a weekly meal-prep date, can also be an exciting and effective method to stay connected and motivated.

In maintaining these connections, flexibility and communication are crucial. Life changes, and so will your support network's needs and dynamics. Open communication about what is or isn't working will help you and your support network adapt and continue providing the support you need.

These relationships and connections provide the encouragement, understanding, and accountability that can make all the difference in maintaining your progress. They remind you that you're in good company and a part of a community; that support is always available, whether through a comforting conversation with a friend or professional advice from a therapist. Keep nurturing these connections, and let them help you sustain the positive changes you've worked so hard to implement.

Chapter 8
Lifestyle Changes For Long-Term Success

"Don't go through life, grow through life."
~ Eric Butterworth

Visualize this: you're at a vibrant market, strolling past stalls bursting with fresh produce, your senses tingling with the colors and scents. As you pick up a ripe, sun-warmed tomato, you think not just of the salads it will enhance but of the joy and fulfillment that comes from choosing foods that nourish your body and soul. This scene isn't just about food shopping — it's about weaving healthy eating into the fabric of a balanced, joyful lifestyle.

In this chapter, we'll dive into how integrating healthy eating into your life is not about restrictions or overwhelming diet rules but about enriching your life, embracing flexibility, and aligning your meals with your values and joys.

8.1 Integrating Healthy Eating into a Balanced Lifestyle

Let's talk about the idea of moving beyond dieting. It's about adopting a holistic approach to health where eating healthy isn't a chore or a list of don'ts but a series of choices that enhance your overall quality of life. Consider integrating foods into your diet that you genuinely enjoy and contribute to your health. It's like marrying pleasure with purpose in every bite.

This approach invites you to listen to your body and respond with foods that satisfy taste and nutritional needs without swinging the pendulum to extremes of overindulgence or restrictive eating.

Flexibility and moderation are your best friends in this pursuit.

It's easy to fall into the trap of rigid dieting rules, which can lead to a yo-yo cycle of restrictive eating and overeating. Instead, embracing flexibility means allowing yourself a piece of chocolate cake at a party without guilt, enjoying it thoroughly, and then simply returning to your usual eating habits the next meal.

It's about balance, not perfection. Moderation allows you to enjoy the foods you love without feeling deprived or going overboard. Think of it as the middle path where you can appreciate all foods in appropriate portions that align with your body's needs.

Incorporating enjoyment and pleasure in eating is crucial.

Food is not just fuel; it's also a delightful source of pleasure, which is rightly so. Preparing and consuming meals should bring joy. This can be achieved by experimenting with new recipes, savoring each meal, and turning dining into a delightful experience rather than just a daily necessity. Whether trying out a new restaurant or cooking a beloved family recipe, enjoying each meal is a celebration of life through food.

Aligning your eating habits with your personal values and goals creates a fulfilling sense of purpose in your dietary choices.

For instance, if environmental sustainability is important to you, you might focus on incorporating more plant-based meals into your diet. If supporting local businesses resonates with you, purchasing from local farmers' markets becomes a part of your routine. These choices allow your meals to reflect your personal convictions, which can enrich your sense of well-being and satisfaction.

Reflective Journaling Prompt

Take a moment to reflect on how your current eating habits align with your lifestyle and values.

- Are there changes you'd like to make to bring more joy or health into your meals?

- How can you introduce more flexibility to your diet?

- Write down a few thoughts on how you can make your meals more enjoyable and aligned with your values.

This exercise is not just about planning but feeling inspired and motivated by the potential for joy and health in your daily meals.

Embracing these concepts transforms eating from a source of stress to one of joy and health. It's about making choices that support your well-being on all levels — physical, emotional, and ethical — and doing so in a natural and enjoyable way. This approach not only sustains your physical health but also enriches your life, making every meal a celebration of your values and desires. As you integrate these concepts into your daily life, remember that each little step contributes to a broader journey toward a harmonious, joyful way of living that cherishes and honors your feelings about food.

8.2 Sleep: The Unsung Hero in Managing Emotional Eating

We often overlook sleep's silent yet profound influence on our lives, especially concerning our eating patterns. Think about the last time you had a poor night's sleep. How did you feel the next day? Chances are, you were not just cranky but also unusually hungry, reaching for snacks or extra coffee to get through the day. This isn't just a coincidence.

Sleep affects our hunger hormones: ghrelin and leptin. Ghrelin signals hunger, and your body makes more of it when you're sleep-deprived. Conversely, leptin tells your brain you're full, but when you're running on little sleep, your leptin levels drop. This hormonal imbalance can increase hunger and appetite, pushing you toward excessive eating or craving high-calorie, sugary foods as quick energy fixes. Improving sleep hygiene can transform your eating habits and overall health.

Start crafting a bedtime routine to signal your body that it's time to wind down.

- This might involve dimming the lights, turning off screens at least an hour before bed to reduce blue light exposure, or
- Indulging in relaxing activities such as taking a warm bath or reading a book.

The key is consistency; you can start with setting your body's internal clock.

- Try going to bed and waking up at the same time every day, which will help improve your sleep quality.

Also, evaluate your sleep environment.

- Is your bedroom conducive to rest?

- Consider factors like room temperature, noise levels, and the comfort of your mattress and pillows.

To significantly enhance your sleep, you can try these:

- Putting on eye masks.
- Investing in comfortable bedding.
- Installing blackout curtains can significantly improve your sleep quality.

Mindfulness for Better Sleep

Including mindfulness practices can also enhance the quality of your sleep, acting as a bridge to peaceful slumber, especially if stress or anxiety frequently keeps you awake.

Why not try a technique

TIPS Mindfulness is about focusing on the present moment and accepting it without judgment. This practice can significantly soothe your mind and alleviate concerns that frequently cause sleeplessness.

- Guided imagery, wherein you envision a tranquil setting or situation.
- This can help you shift your focus away from stress.

Similarly, *progressive muscle relaxation*, which involves tensing and relaxing different muscle groups, can reduce physical tension and promote relaxation.

Another effective method is the *practice of gratitude*. Spend a few minutes before bed reflecting on or jotting down things you were grateful for throughout the day. This practice can shift your mindset from stress to positivity, making it easier to fall asleep.

The impact of good sleep on well-being extends beyond just feeling rested. Quality sleep supports various aspects of your health, such as improving your immune system and reducing the risk of chronic conditions like heart disease, obesity, and diabetes. Emotionally, adequate sleep can improve mood, enhance cognitive functions, and increase energy levels, which can help you manage emotions and stress, reducing the likelihood of emotional eating.

Moreover, when you're well-rested, you're more likely to have the energy and motivation to make thoughtful food choices and engage in physical activity, both of which are crucial for maintaining a healthy lifestyle.

So, as you consider the lifestyle changes that support your goals of managing emotional eating and living healthily, don't underestimate the power of a good night's sleep. It's not merely about closing your eyes and lying down; it's an active and valuable participant in your health and well-being, silently but significantly influencing your daily life and decisions.

As you continue exploring and implementing better health strategies, let sleep be a cornerstone of your efforts, supporting and enhancing your journey toward a balanced, healthy life.

8.3 Time Management Strategies for Stress Reduction

In the whirlwind of daily life, especially when juggling roles as a parent, professional, or partner, finding a calm moment can sometimes feel like searching for a needle in a haystack. But what if you could weave these calm moments into your day more seamlessly?

It's all about smart time management, and believe it or not, it can significantly reduce stress and maintain a healthier relationship with food. When stress levels drop, so do those impulsive trips to the pantry.

Let's explore how prioritizing self-care, setting healthy boundaries, efficiently using your time, and taking mindful breaks can help you transform your daily routine from chaotic to harmonious.

STRATEGY *Prioritizing self-care* is a crucial step toward a balanced life. Think of self-care as an appointment with your most important client: yourself. It deserves a non-negotiable spot in your calendar, just like any crucial meeting. Whether it's a 20-minute walk, a quick meditation session, or simply sitting down with a cup of tea and a book, ensure these activities are scheduled into your day.

It's tempting to think of self-care as a luxury you'll get to 'when there's time' but let's flip that narrative. Making time for self-care enables you to handle everything else on your plate more effectively. It recharges your batteries, reduces stress, and can help curb emotional eating by keeping your mood more stable.

Setting boundaries is another key strategy. This might mean saying no to extra commitments that don't align with your priorities or delegating tasks at home or work. Boundaries help you avoid overloading your schedule, which can lead to stress and burnout. If you're clear about your boundaries, you're more likely to maintain them, reducing tension and modeling healthy behavior for those around you. It's about respecting your own limits and ensuring others do too.

For instance, if late-night emails are eating into your downtime, establish a cut-off time after which you don't check your work email. Communicate this boundary clearly to your colleagues or clients to set expectations.

Efficient time use is all about working smarter, not harder.

- Start by identifying the times of day when you're most productive.

- Are you a morning person who can power through reports before lunch, or do you find your stride in the afternoon?

- Coordinate your most challenging tasks with these peak periods to maximize your natural energy cycles.

- Also, consider tools or techniques that can streamline your tasks. It could be a meal planning app that saves you time at the grocery store or batching similar tasks together to reduce the time spent ramping up for different activities.

Being efficient with your time can decrease the feeling of racing against the clock, often a precursor to stress and stress-related snacking.

Encouraging regular, *mindful break*s throughout your day is essential. These aren't just pauses; they're moments to reset and center yourself. It could be as simple as taking a few deep breaths between meetings or enjoying a quiet moment before the household wakes up. These breaks are vital for mental clarity and emotional equilibrium.

- They give you a chance to step back and assess how you're feeling, which can be particularly helpful if you're prone to stress eating.

- Use these breaks to check in with yourself: How are you feeling?

- What do you need at this moment?

These mindful breaks can help you make more conscious choices about food and everything else in your day.

Integrating these time management strategies into your life isn't just about keeping your schedule under control; it's about creating a lifestyle that supports your mental and physical health. By prioritizing self-care, setting clear boundaries, using your time efficiently, and taking mindful breaks, you're setting the stage for a less stressful, more fulfilling daily experience.

This approach doesn't just help manage stress — it enhances your overall well-being, making you more resilient against the stressors that life throws your way.

8.4 Setting Goals for the Future: Beyond Emotional Eating

Imagine a version of yourself who feels at peace with food, where meals are a source of nourishment and joy rather than stress or guilt. Picture a day when emotional eating doesn't dictate your choices, and you feel empowered to enjoy life's pleasures beyond the dining table. This vision of your future self isn't just a daydream; it's a potential reality that begins with setting thoughtful, clear goals. These goals act as beacons, guiding you through the fog of daily struggles and illuminating your path toward a healthier, more fulfilled self.

When setting these goals, it's crucial to employ a method that ensures they are clear, achievable, and tailored to support your specific needs and aspirations.

This is where **SMART** goals come into play, a strategy renowned for effectiveness in various settings, from business to personal development. S-M-A-R-T is an acronym for Specific, Measurable, Achievable, Relevant, and Time-bound. Each goal you set should pass these criteria.

For example, instead of setting a vague goal like "eat healthier," a SMART version would be, "I will include at least a serving of vegetables and a serving of fruits in my lunch and dinner, five days a week, for the next month." This goal is specific (two servings of vegetables), measurable (you can count the servings), achievable (it's a reasonable adjustment), relevant (it aligns with your aim to eat healthier), and time-bound (set for the next month).

Incorporating flexibility into your goal setting is just as important. Life is unpredictable, and rigid goals can sometimes set you up for frustration and disappointment. Allow your goals to have breathing room. Suppose you face a particularly hectic week where preparing meals is challenging. In that case, adjusting your goal to fit your current situation is okay — maybe you can switch to high-quality store-bought salads for a few days. Flexibility in your goals helps you maintain progress without feeling defeated by unforeseen changes or challenges.

Celebrating your progress is vital. No matter how small, every step forward is a piece of the puzzle in your overall growth. Did you choose a healthy snack over junk food three times this week? Celebrate it! These celebrations reinforce positive behavior and boost your motivation to continue. They remind you that progress isn't just about reaching the final goal but valuing the process and growth along the way. It's about acknowledging the effort and change that each small decision represents and how they collectively steer your life in the direction you desire.

By envisioning your future self, setting SMART goals, allowing flexibility, and celebrating every bit of progress, you arm yourself with a powerful strategy to move beyond emotional eating. You create a framework that supports growth, adapts to change, and recognizes achievement, paving the way for a future where food is joy, and your life is full of health and happiness.

As you continue to apply these principles, remember that each goal, adjustment, and celebration is a stepping stone to a better eating pattern and a more prosperous, more vibrant life.

8.5 The Quick-Start 1-Week Mindful Eating Meal Plan

Embarking on a mindful eating practice isn't just about changing what you eat; it's about transforming how you relate to food. It's about turning each meal into an opportunity for presence, gratitude, and enjoyment. Let's start with a quick refresher on the principles of mindful eating.

It's about engaging fully with the experience of eating, noticing the flavors, textures, and sensations, and honoring your body's hunger and fullness cues without judgment.

To help you integrate these principles into your daily life, let's dive into a 1-week mindful eating plan. Each day focuses on a specific theme related to mindful eating, such as gratitude, savoring, and variety, ensuring that you not only nourish your body but also enrich your eating experience.

This is NOT a diet plan — there are no restrictions on the foods you eat; remember that moderation is key. It's about nourishing your body and enjoying your meal, while practicing mindful eating to minimize and keep emotional eating at bay. Here's how you can structure your week (you can also download a digital copy of this 1-week Mindful Eating Plan, further below).

Day 1: Gratitude

You can start the day with a smoothie topped with a variety of fruits and seeds. As you prepare and eat your meal, think about each ingredient's journey to your bowl; the sun and soil that nurtured the fruits, the farmers who harvested them, and the journey they took to your kitchen. Expressing gratitude for these elements can deepen your appreciation for your food, enhancing your eating experience.

Meal Suggestions:

- **Breakfast**: Scrambled eggs with spinach and whole-grain toast.
  - Advice: Start your day with a balanced breakfast to stabilize blood sugar levels and prevent cravings later on.

- **Lunch**: Quinoa salad with mixed greens, cherry tomatoes, cucumbers, and grilled chicken.
  - Advice: Eat slowly and mindfully, focusing on the flavors and textures of each bite.
- **Dinner**: Baked salmon with roasted sweet potatoes and steamed broccoli.
  - Advice: Pause halfway through your meal to check in with your hunger levels. Stop eating when you feel satisfied, not overly full.

Day 2: Savoring

Choose a meal that you truly love and take the time to eat it slowly, savoring each bite. It could be a creamy risotto or a perfectly cooked steak. With each forkful, focus on the different flavors and textures. Notice how they combine and contrast, and fully immerse yourself in the pleasure of eating.

Meal Suggestions:

- Breakfast: Overnight oats with Greek yogurt, berries, and a sprinkle of nuts.
  - Advice: Practice gratitude before eating each meal. Reflect on the nourishment and enjoyment your food provides.
- Lunch: Whole-grain wrap with hummus, avocado, lettuce, and sliced turkey.
  - Advice: Avoid distractions while eating. Turn off screens and focus solely on your meal.
- Dinner: Stir-fried tofu with mixed vegetables and brown rice.

- Advice: Engage in light activity, such as a short walk, after dinner to support digestion and prevent mindless snacking.

Day 3: Mindful Snacking

Prepare a plate of snacks — nuts, chopped fruits, cheese, and crackers. Sit down and eat each snack individually, focusing on each piece's taste and texture. This practice can help you enjoy the quality of your food rather than mindlessly munching.

Meal Suggestions:

- Breakfast: Smoothie bowl topped with granola, banana slices, and chia seeds.
  - Advice: Stay hydrated throughout the day. Drink water or herbal tea between meals to stay mindful of thirst cues.
- Lunch: Lentil soup with a side of whole-grain bread.
  - Advice: Practice deep breathing or a short mindfulness meditation before eating to center yourself and reduce stress.
- Dinner: Grilled chicken breast with roasted vegetables and quinoa.
  - Advice: Plan your meals and snacks ahead of time to avoid impulsive eating decisions.

Day 4: Colorful Meals

Create a meal that includes as many colors as possible. A vibrant salad with greens, red peppers, orange carrots, blueberries, and a sprinkle of nuts looks appealing and involves different flavors and textures. Eating a visually appealing meal can enhance your enjoyment and encourage you to eat more mindfully.

Meal Suggestions:

- Breakfast: Whole-grain toast with almond butter and sliced apples.
  - Advice: Choose whole, minimally processed foods whenever possible to support overall well-being.
- Lunch: Chickpea salad with cucumbers, tomatoes, feta cheese, and a lemon-tahini dressing.
  - Advice: Practice self-compassion and let go of guilt associated with food choices. Focus on nourishment rather than restriction.
- Dinner: Baked cod with steamed green beans and wild rice.
  - Advice: Eat in a calm environment, free from distractions or stressful stimuli.

Day 5: New Recipe Day

Try a new recipe that involves an unfamiliar ingredient or cooking method. The novelty can heighten your awareness and focus as you cook and eat, making the meal an exploratory experience.

Meal Suggestions:

- Breakfast: Greek yogurt with honey, sliced almonds, and fresh berries.
  - Advice: Pay attention to portion sizes. Use smaller plates and bowls to prevent overeating.

- Lunch: Whole-grain pasta with marinara sauce and a side of roasted vegetables.
    - Advice: Acknowledge and address emotional triggers without turning to food. Practice alternative coping mechanisms such as journaling or talking to a friend.
- Dinner: Grilled shrimp skewers with a mixed green salad and quinoa.
    - Advice: Practice mindful eating by chewing slowly and savoring each bite. Notice how different foods make you feel.

Day 6: Silent Meal

Have a meal in silence, free from distractions like TV or smartphones. Use this time to really tune into your food and your body's signals. Eating without distractions helps you realize when you've eaten enough and feel full, thus reducing the likelihood of overeating.

Meal Suggestions:

- Breakfast: Chia seed pudding with sliced kiwi and a sprinkle of coconut flakes.
    - Advice: Stay attuned to hunger and fullness signals. Stop eating when you feel comfortably satisfied.
- Lunch: Brown rice bowl with black beans, avocado, salsa, and grilled chicken.
    - Advice: Focus on the present moment while eating. Avoid thoughts of past or future worries.
- Dinner: Grilled steak with roasted Brussels sprouts and a side of quinoa.

- Advice: Practice positive self-talk and affirmations related to your body and eating habits.

Day 7: Reflection

Choose your favorite meal from the week and prepare it again. While eating, reflect on your experiences throughout the week. What did you learn? Did some practices make the meal more enjoyable? Use these insights to adjust and refine your mindful eating practices.

Meal Suggestions:

- Breakfast: Whole-grain waffles with Greek yogurt, sliced peaches, and a drizzle of honey.
  - Advice: Reflect on your progress throughout the week. Celebrate small victories and moments of mindfulness.
- Lunch: Tuna salad lettuce wraps with cherry tomatoes and cucumber slices.
  - Advice: Be gentle with yourself. Remember that progress takes time, and each mindful choice adds up over time.
- Dinner: Grilled vegetable platter with hummus, whole-grain pita, and a side of quinoa.
  - Advice: End your day with gratitude. Reflect on the positive aspects of your mindful eating journey.

Simple Tips

Preparation is vital in mindful eating. Plan your meals in advance to ensure you have all the necessary ingredients. Try simple, nourishing recipes that don't require complicated preparations but are rich in flavors and textures.

For instance, a hearty vegetable soup or a quinoa salad with mixed greens, dried cranberries, and a lemon-tahini dressing can be both satisfying and simple to prepare.

Scan this QR code or use the link to download a digital copy of this chart:

Quick Start 1-Week Mindful Meal Plan

DAY	BREAKFAST	LUNCH	DINNER
Day-1 Gratitude	Scrambled eggs with spinach and whole-grain toast. Start your day with a balanced breakfast to stabilize blood sugar levels and prevent cravings later on.	Quinoa salad with mixed greens, cherry tomatoes, cucumbers, and grilled chicken. Eat slowly and mindfully, ocusing on the flavors and textures of each bite.	Baked salmon with roasted sweet potatoes and steamed broccoli. Pause halfway through your meal to check in with your hunger levels. Stop eating when you feel satisfied, not overly full.
Day-2 Savoring	Overnight oats with Greek yogurt, berries, and a sprinkle of nuts. Practice gratitude before eating each meal. Reflect on the nourishment and enjoyment your food provides.	Whole-grain wrap with hummus, avocado, lettuce, and sliced turkey. Avoid distractions while eating. Turn off screens and focus solely on your meal.	Stir-fried tofu with mixed vegetables and brown rice. Engage in light activity, such as a short walk, after dinner to support digestion and prevent mindless snacking.
Day-3 Mindful Snacking	Smoothie bowl topped with granola, banana slices, and chia seeds. Stay hydrated throughout the day. Drink water or herbal tea between meals to stay mindful of thirst cues.	Lentil soup with a side of whole-grain bread. Practice deep breathing or a short mindfulness meditation before eating to center yourself and reduce stress.	Grilled chicken breast with roasted vegetables and quinoa. Plan your meals and snacks ahead of time to avoid impulsive eating decisions.
Day-4 Colorful Meals	Whole-grain toast with almond butter and sliced apples. Choose whole, minimally processed foods whenever possible to support overall well-being.	Chickpea salad with cucumbers, tomatoes, feta cheese, and a lemon-tahini dressing. Practice self-compassion and let go of guilt associated with food choices. Focus on nourishment rather than restriction.	Baked cod with steamed green beans and wild rice. Eat in a calm environment, free from distractions or stressful stimuli.
Day-5 New Recipe Day	Greek yogurt with honey, sliced almonds, and fresh berries. Pay attention to portion sizes. Use smaller plates and bowls to prevent overeating.	Whole-grain pasta with marinara sauce and a side of roasted vegetables. Acknowledge and address emotional triggers without]turning to food. Practice alternative coping mechanisms such as journaling or talking to a friend.	Grilled shrimp skewers with a mixed green salad and quinoa. Practice mindful eating by chewing slowly and savoring each bite. Notice how different foods make you feel.
Day-6 Silent Meal	Chia seed pudding with sliced kiwi and a sprinkle of coconut flakes. Stay attuned to hunger and fullness signals. Stop eating when you feel comfortably satisfied.	Brown rice bowl with black beans, avocado, salsa, and grilled chicken. Focus on the present moment while eating. Avoid thoughts of past or future worries.	Grilled steak with roasted Brussels sprouts and a side of quinoa. Practice positive self-talk and affirmations related to your body and eating habits.
Day-7 Reflection	Whole-grain waffles with Greek yogurt, sliced peaches, and \a drizzle of honey. Reflect on your progress throughout the week. Celebrate small victories and moments of mindfulness.	Tuna salad lettuce wraps with cherry tomatoes and cucumber slices. Be gentle with yourself. Remember that progress takes time, and each mindful choice adds up over time.	Grilled vegetable platter with hummus, whole-grain pita, and a side of quinoa. End your day with gratitude. Reflect on the positive aspects of your mindful eating journey.

Reflection and Adjustment

At the end of each day, take a few minutes to reflect on your eating experiences. What did you notice? How did the practices affect your mood or your satisfaction with your meals? Write down your thoughts and feelings. This reflection provides valuable insights into your eating habits and helps you understand which practices you might want to continue, adjust, or change.

This one-week eating plan is about weaving mindfulness into your approach to food and your eating habits. It's an invitation to slow down, savor, and reconnect with the joys of eating. Remember that these practices aren't rigid rules but flexible guidelines designed to enhance your eating experience and nourish your body and mind.

8.6 Holistic Approach to Healing

Let's take a moment to consolidate and remind ourselves of everything we've learned so far. We've delved into a holistic approach to conquering emotional eating, addressing it from every angle. Here's a quick recap of what we've learned:

Understand Emotional Eating:

Recognize the triggers and patterns of emotional eating. Emotional eating entails using food to cope with stress, boredom, sadness, or other emotions. Identify specific emotions or situations that commonly lead to emotional eating episodes.

Mindfulness and Awareness:

Engage in mindfulness to heighten your awareness of your thoughts, feelings, and behaviors around food. Mindfulness techniques such as meditation, deep breathing, and mindful eating can help. Pay attention to physical hunger cues rather than emotional hunger cues. Emotional hunger typically arises suddenly and targets specific foods (such as craving comfort foods), whereas physical hunger builds up gradually and can be satisfied with various foods.

Address Emotional Triggers:

Cultivate restorative coping methods to manage emotions. This may include journaling, talking to a therapist or counselor, practicing relaxation techniques, or engaging in creative outlets like art or music. Learn to identify and process emotions in a healthy way rather than using food as a primary coping mechanism.

Nutrition and Balanced Eating:

Focus on nourishing your body with a well-rounded and diverse diet rich in lean proteins, healthy fats, fruits, vegetables, and whole grains. Avoid strict diets or food restrictions that can result in a sense of deprivation and trigger emotional overeating. Practice mindful eating by paying attention to hunger and fullness cues and slowing down eating while enjoying and savoring each bite.

Physical Activity:

Incorporate regular physical activity into your routine. Exercise boosts your mood and self-esteem and reduces stress, all of which promote healthier eating habits. Choose activities you enjoy, whether walking, yoga, dancing, or strength training.

Sleep and Stress Management:

Prioritizing quality sleep is vital in regulating hunger hormones and overall well-being. Practice stress management techniques such as deep breathing, progressive muscle relaxation, or mindfulness meditation to reduce stress levels and prevent emotional eating triggers.

Social Support and Connection:

Seek support from friends, family, or support groups who understand what you are going through and provide encouragement throughout your journey and accountability. Get connected with people who may share similar goals and experiences so that you feel less isolated and more motivated.

Self-Compassion and Forgiveness:

Be kind to yourself and practice self-compassion. Recognize that the healing process requires time to forgive yourself for past slip-ups or mistakes related to emotional eating. These experiences can lead to learning and personal growth.

Professional Guidance:

Consult with a registered dietitian, therapist, or holistic health practitioner who specializes in this area. Collaborate with professionals to create a customized plan that caters to your personal challenges, needs, and goals.

By embracing holistic healing, we embark on a journey of self-discovery and transformation. It's not just about temporary fixes or quick solutions; it's about nurturing sustainable changes that resonate with our unique needs and values.

Chapter 9
Happier Life Beyond Emotional Eating

"The purpose of our lives is to be happy."
~ Dalai Lama

Let's visualize yourself at a crossroads in a lush, captivating forest. Numerous paths stretch out before you, each winding through majestic trees and vanishing into misty, unexplored destinations. The decision to choose a path might seem overwhelming, as each step into the unknown brings a mix of anticipation and unease.

This forest mirrors the journey you're on, transcending emotional eating. It's not merely about selecting a path but about embracing the journey itself. With all its twists and turns, this journey is a profound voyage of self-discovery and growth, offering as much beauty and fulfillment as it challenges.

9.1 Embracing Change: The Journey of Self-Discovery and Growth

Embracing the Journey

Embracing change isn't just about adapting to new routines; it's about seeing these changes as gateways to deeper self-awareness and personal growth. Each step you take to overcome emotional eating is a testament to your inner strength, offering a mirror into your inner world, reflecting back your strengths, fears, and the boundless potential for transformation. It's about peeling back layers you might not have known existed, uncovering desires and wounds, and nurturing them with kindness.

This process is ongoing; there's no final destination or perfect state of being. Instead, it's a continuous unfolding journey that offers as much beauty and fulfillment as it brings challenges. Walk this path with an open heart, to learn more about yourself and how you relate to the world around you.

Overcoming Fear of Change

Change can be scary; it pushes you out of your comfort zone and challenges your sense of security. What if you saw these changes not as challenges but as chances for personal development and growth? Start by identifying what change scares you. Is it the fear of failure, or perhaps the fear of losing a part of your identity tied up with your eating habits? Once you pinpoint these fears, you can start to address them directly.

Techniques such as journaling can help you articulate and confront these fears. Write about what change means to you, what it brings up inside you, and how you might benefit from embracing it. Visualization can also be a powerful tool. Picture yourself effectively navigating a change, experiencing empowerment and rejuvenation. This mental visualization practice can boost your confidence and reduce anxiety about the changes you're making.

The Role of Resilience

Resilience refers to your capacity to recover from challenges and setbacks, and it's a crucial quality to cultivate to reach your goal. It's about adopting a mindset that sees difficulties as surmountable and failures as lessons. When a setback in your eating habits occurs, instead of succumbing to self-criticism, ask yourself, 'What can I learn from this?' It might reveal the need for more supportive structures or highlight unresolved emotions that require attention.

Strengthening resilience also involves self-care practices that keep you grounded and balanced, such as mindfulness, regular physical activity, and connections with supportive friends or family. These practices help you recover from setbacks more quickly and fortify you against future challenges.

Celebrating Each Step

Every small victory along this journey deserves recognition and celebration, a testament to your strength and progress. Did you choose a healthy snack over an emotional binge? Celebrate that choice. Did you take time to meditate or relax instead of turning to food when stressed? Give yourself credit for that progress.

Celebrating these victories, big or small, reinforces positive behaviors and boosts your morale. It also helps to keep a 'victory log' — a special notebook where you jot down your successes. Over time, this log will fill up with reminders of your strength and progress, serving as a powerful motivator to keep going, especially on tougher days.

Victory Log Exercise

ACTION Start your victory log today. Grab a notebook or open a new digital document and write down one small victory from your day. It could be anything from cooking a healthy meal to resisting a binge to recognizing a trigger. Make this a daily habit, and watch as your log becomes a testament to your growing strength and resilience.

Navigating the changes that come with overcoming emotional eating is no small feat. It requires courage, commitment, and a lot of self-compassion.

Every step you take is not just about leaving unhealthy habits behind; it's about moving closer to a version of yourself that is healthier, happier, and deeply attuned to your own needs and aspirations.

By embracing holistic healing, we embark on a journey of self-discovery and transformation. It's not just about temporary fixes or quick solutions; it's about nurturing sustainable changes that resonate with our unique needs and values.

9.2 Beyond the Book: Continuing Your Journey Toward a Happier You

Envision your life as a beautiful garden. Just as a garden continually grows and changes, requiring new seeds, regular watering, and care to thrive, your journey toward a happier, healthier self is ongoing. The pages of this book are akin to the essential tools and initial seeds you need, but real growth happens when you continue to nurture your garden with new knowledge and experiences.

Lifelong learning is not just crucial; it's exciting — so try to embrace it. It means remaining curious and open, always looking for new ways to understand yourself and the world around you. Whether it's picking up psychology books to better understand your mind, attending workshops about nutrition, or simply trying out new activities that push you out of your comfort zone, every new piece of knowledge adds depth to your life.

Let's discuss resources that can help you grow beyond this book. There are countless books, websites, blogs and articles out there that can offer new insights and strategies for managing emotional eating. Additionally, consider courses — many community colleges and online platforms offer classes on nutrition, wellness, and psychology that are accessible and can deepen your understanding of the themes we've touched upon.

Patience and persistence are your allies. Remember, growth is rarely linear. There are days when everything seems to click, and you feel like you're making huge strides. Then, there might be days or even weeks when progress feels slow or you feel like you're backsliding. It's all part of the process. The key is to keep pushing forward and to stay committed to your growth despite the setbacks. Celebrate the small victories, learn from the challenges, and remind yourself that every day offers a new opportunity to move closer to your goals.

Finally, I encourage you to share your experiences and engage with others who are on similar journeys. Whether joining online forums, participating in local support groups, or simply sharing your story with friends, connecting with others can provide invaluable support. Learning how others navigate similar challenges can provide fresh strategies or insights and reassure you that you're not facing this alone. Plus, sharing your journey can be incredibly empowering. It not only helps others but also reinforces your own commitment to your growth. So, reach out, connect, and grow together.

As we wrap up this chapter, think of it not as an end but as an invitation to continue exploring, learning, and connecting. You've equipped yourself with foundational knowledge and strategies, but the road ahead is rich with potential for further growth and deeper understanding. Keep nurturing your garden, seeking new learning opportunities, and connecting with others. This ongoing process is where the true joy and beauty of transformation lie.

Keeping The Recovery Path Alive

Now you have everything you need to conquer emotional eating, it's time to pass on your new found knowledge and show other readers where they can find the same help.

By simply leaving your honest opinion of this book on Amazon, you'll help others who want to break free from emotional eating by showing them where they can find the information they're looking for.

Simply scan this QR code to leave your review on Amazon or go to: https://amzn.to/4bgXcpW

'Emotional Eating - Why We Do It & How To Beat It' is kept alive when we pass on our knowledge – and you're helping me to do just that. Your kind help is deeply appreciated.

> "Happiness doesn't result from what we get, but from what we give."
>
> ~ Ben Carson

Conclusion

Dear readers,

Now that we've come to the end of our journey together in this book, I want to reflect on the incredible path we've traveled. From the initial steps of understanding the roots of emotional eating and identifying our triggers, building resilient strategies, and building a healthy relationship with food to finally integrating mindful eating into a balanced and joyful lifestyle — what a journey it has been!

We've explored the importance of self-compassion, recognizing that being kind to ourselves is not just a luxury but a necessity. We've learned to embrace mindfulness, to be present with our food, and to enjoy every bite, free from the chains of diet culture. Together, we've addressed not just our emotional needs but also our physical ones, fostering a positive body image and balancing our nutrition with care and understanding.

As you continue on your path, remember that this isn't the end of your journey but a beautiful ongoing process of self-discovery and growth. Be curious, remain receptive to novel ideas, and continue enhancing your life with knowledge. Whether through books, workshops, or conversations with peers, every piece of new learning can help you refine your strategies for managing emotional eating.

I encourage you to take a small but powerful step today, toward your ultimate goal. Start by bringing full awareness to your next meal, or spare ten minutes tonight to record and reflect on any emotional trigger for the day. These minor actions can result in significant transformations.

Keep in mind that every journey comes with its highs and lows. Setbacks aren't failures; they're part of the learning process. They make you stronger and more resilient. Keep pushing forward with patience and persistence, and know that you are capable of overcoming the challenges that come your way.

Thank you for allowing me to be a part of your journey. Your courage in facing and working through emotional eating is truly inspiring. As you continue to make strides, I hope you'll share your story. Whether it's on social media, a blog, or just among friends, your story has the power to inspire and encourage others who are fighting the same battle.

Finally, I want to leave you with a message of hope and solidarity. I believe wholeheartedly in your ability to transform your life and find a happier, more balanced relationship with food. Here's to moving forward, embracing change, and enjoying every step toward a healthier, happier you.

With all my gratitude and best wishes,

Kitty Barrett

References

1. Better Health Channel. (n.d.). Emotional Eating and How to Stop It. https://www.betterhealth.vic.gov.au/health/healthyliving/physical-activity-setting-yourself-goals

2. Emotion Matters. (2018). How Does Social Media Influence Body Image?. https://emotionmatters.co.uk/2018/10/04/how-does-social-media-influence-body-image/

3. Forbes. (2022). 4 Tools For Developing Critical Media Literacy Skills From NAMLE. https://www.forbes.com/sites/meimeifox/2022/12/05/4-tools-for-developing-critical-media-literacy-skills-from-namle/

4. Germer, C. K., Siegel, R. D., & Fulton, P. R. (Eds.). (2013). Mindfulness and psychotherapy (2nd ed.). Guilford Press.

5. Harvard Health Publishing. (n.d.). Why stress causes people to overeat. Harvard Health Publishing. https://www.health.harvard.edu/staying-healthy/why-stress-causes-people-to-overeat

6. Harvard T.H. Chan School of Public Health. (n.d.). Mindful Eating. The Nutrition Source. https://www.hsph.harvard.edu/nutritionsource/mindful-eating/

7. Harvard T.H. Chan School of Public Health. (2022). The Nutrition Source. https://www.hsph.harvard.edu/nutritionsource/

8. Hartley, R. (n.d.). Emotional Hunger vs. Physical Hunger: How to Tell The Difference. Rachel Hartley Nutrition. https://www.rachaelhartleynutrition.com/blog/emotional-hunger-vs-physical-hunger

9. Healthline. (n.d.). Emotional Eating and How to Stop It. https://www.healthline.com/health/emotional-eating

10. Healthline. (n.d.). Mindful Eating 101 — A Beginner's Guide. https://www.healthline.com/nutrition/mindful-eating-guide

11. HelpGuide.org. (n.d.). Emotional Eating and How to Stop It. https://www.helpguide.org/articles/diets/emotional-eating.htm

12. Intuitive Eating. (n.d.). 10 Principles of Intuitive Eating. https://www.intuitiveeating.org/10-principles-of-intuitive-eating/

13. Jamie Spannhake. (n.d.). Reduce Stress with Effective Time Management. https://www.jamiespannhake.com/blogs/calm-in-the-chaos-blog/reduce-stress-with-effective-time-management

14. Lall Nutrition. (n.d.). Client Case Study – Resolving Emotional Eating. https://lallnutrition.com/client-case-study-resolving-emotional-eating/

15. LinkedIn. (n.d.). The Role of Self-Compassion in Recovery. https://www.linkedin.com/pulse/role-self-compassion-recovery-recovery-unplugged-r2whc

16. Mayo Clinic. (n.d.). Weight loss: Gain control of emotional eating. https://www.mayoclinic.org/healthy-lifestyle/weight-loss/in-depth/weight-loss/art-20047342

17. Medium. (n.d.). 10 Holistic Self-Care Practices & Strategies for a healthy mind, body & soul. https://medium.com/@theeasywisdom/10-holistic-self-care-practices-strategies-for-a-healthy-mind-body-soul-682b6428b684

18. Michaels, R. J., & Smith, M. F. (2014). Stress and Eating Behaviors. PMC - NCBI. National Center for Biotechnology Information. https://www.ncbi.nlm.nih.gov/pmc/articles/PMC4214609/

19. National Alliance on Mental Health. (2019). The Importance of Community and Mental Health. https://www.nami.org/Blogs/NAMI-Blog/November-2019/The-Importance-of-Community-and-Mental-Health

20. National Institute of Mental Health. (n.d.). Eating Disorders: About More Than Food. https://www.nimh.nih.gov/health/publications/eating-disorders

21. NCBI. (n.d.). BodyPositive? A critical exploration of the body positive movement. https://www.ncbi.nlm.nih.gov/pmc/articles/PMC9589104/

22. NCBI. (2020). Food and mood: how do diet and nutrition affect mental wellbeing?. https://www.ncbi.nlm.nih.gov/pmc/articles/PMC7322666/

23. NCBI. (2020). Role of Physical Activity on Mental Health and Well-Being. https://www.ncbi.nlm.nih.gov/pmc/articles/PMC9902068/

24. Positive Psychology. (n.d.). 16 Effective Stress-Management Activities and Worksheets. https://positivepsychology.com/stress-management-activities-worksheets/

25. Prevention Magazine. (n.d.). How Mindful Eating Helped Me Lose Weight And Love Food. https://www.prevention.com/weight-loss/a20472857/how-mindful-eating-helped-me-lose-weight-and-love-food/

26. Simmons, A. (2012). Eating Well: Understanding Physical and Emotional Hunger. National Library of Medicine. https://pubmed.ncbi.nlm.nih.gov/22281161/

27. Sublime Reflection. (n.d.). How to Keep an Emotional Eating Food Journal {Download}. https://sublimereflection.com/emotional-eating-food-journal/

28. Taylor, S. R. (2020). The body is not an apology: The power of radical self-love (2nd ed.). Berrett-Koehler Publishers.

29. Tribole, E., & Resch, E. (2020). Intuitive eating: A revolutionary anti-diet approach (4th ed.). St. Martin's Essentials.

30. Verywell Fit. (n.d.). How to Say No to a Food Pusher. https://www.verywellfit.com/how-to-say-no-to-food-pushers-3495964

31. Verywell Health. (n.d.). The Psychology (and Politics) of Food Labels. https://www.verywellhealth.com/intuitive-eating-5272316

32. WebMD. (n.d.). Mental Health Benefits of Journaling. https://www.webmd.com/mental-health/mental-health-benefits-of-journaling

33. Well Being Trust. (n.d.). 10 Ways to Practice Body Positivity. https://wellbeingtrust.org/bewell/10-ways-to-practice-body-positivity

34. Whole30. (n.d.). Set Boundaries Around Food, Alcohol, and Table Talk. https://whole30.com/article/set-boundaries-around-food-alcohol-and-table-talk

Printed in Great Britain
by Amazon